# JED

## The Memoirs of Gerald Cook
### Legendary Cowboy and Storyteller of Deep Creek

## As Told by Gerald Cook
### Written by Marilyn Cook Linares

### Edited by Nancy Morrison

Printed and Published in the United States of America
by Word Wright Publishing, LP, Billings, MT
ISBN-10: 0-9966034-4-1
ISBN-13: 978-0-9966034-4-7
Library of Congress Control Number: 2017908913
First printing.

*JED* details the unique memoirs and events of Gerald Cook,
a 98-year-old, life-long resident and legendary cowboy,
rancher, and storyteller of Ibapah, Utah,
as told by Gerald "Jed" Cook
to his daughter, Marilyn Cook Linares.

Photograph on cover by Joyce Cook.
Gerald Cook, Peek-A-Boo, and Tobe. Circa 1950.

Nancy Morrison, Editor, Designer, and Typesetter
PO Box 81633
Billings, MT 59108
Proofing by Linda Grosskopf, Editor, *Western Ag Reporter*

For additional copies of this book, contact:
Marilyn Linares
HC 61 Box 6042
Ibapah, UT 84034

$20 (includes S/H)

"I was never much good at anything in my life
'cept for horses and music."
~ Jed Cook ~

# Dedication

To the gentle hand that guides men,
horses, and me.

# Contents

# Foreword

I am an old woman… and yet relatively young by my father's standards. My dad, for whom I've written this book, is the 98-year-old, living, breathing, legendary cowboy and historian of Ibapah.

I've spent most of my life in Ibapah, Utah. I can't count the times when I've heard someone say, "Ibapah? I've never heard of that. Where is it?" My rote explanation is that it's a small ranching community on the Utah/Nevada line. While Ibapah is certainly small in populace, it is starkly contrasted in the vastness of expanse of land and space between ranches.

Ibapah valley, tucked away from the rest of the world, is surrounded on three sides by awe-inspiring mountain ranges.

The Deep Creek range, bordering the east, is a rugged set of mountains including Ibapah Peak, which has an elevation of over 12,000 feet. The boomtown of Gold Hill lies in the northern end of the range. The Schellbourne Mountains, including Tippett Mountains and Chin Creek, create a border some 30 miles to the west.

My dad's beloved Pleasant Valley or South Mountains, where he spent the majority of his childhood days herding sheep, lie to the south. The infamous Bonneville Salt Flats and the glittering casino border town of Wendover lie some 60 miles to the north. Spring Creek, Dad's Creek, Fifteen Mile Creek, and other smaller tributaries meander through the big valley, irrigating meadows and ranches along the way.

The very hearty people of the Goshute were the first inhabitants of the area. In the early 1800s, the first white men seeking adventure arrived. My paternal grandmother's father immigrated to the area and homesteaded in 1872. My father's father happened along not long after, and that's where Jed's story truly begins.

Mention of Wendover as a reference point usually sparks recognition, and so people get a general idea of where Ibapah is. The word originates from the Goshute language loosely interpreted as "white or clay-colored water." The community is also commonly known as Deep Creek and called as such by longtime residents and old-timers. I am fourth generation in this ranching community on the edges of the Goshute Indian Reservation. I often tell people that I've bloomed where I was planted, living most of my life in Deep Creek. I am a mother of three and a grandmother of three. I taught school in the two-room school house in Ibapah for the past 30 years... but enough about me.

The memories that follow belong to my dad. He is a living Pecos Bill tall tale character straight out of a bygone era and he is my hero. I've scribed his words as "straight-out-of-the-horse's-mouth" as possible, in his simple cowboy vernacular, to maintain the integrity of his true character and voice.

He's never liked to be recorded, so after listening to a few anecdotes, I'd hurry home and feverishly jot down the notes in a dog-eared, green, Mead three-subject notebook. The stories written there, while memorable and poignant, were, at best, disconnected and out of time order. Over the years, I have written and rewritten again to place them in chronological order and connect the memoirs in a meaningful way.

Most of his life Dad has walked with the iconic, hard-knocks, cowboy bowed legs. When asked about his bowed legs, his response was, "I didn't get these legs from sitting on chairs."

In 2012, he fell and broke his left hip, and when it healed, it changed the shape of him. His body currently closely resembles a rather lop-sided capital S. Presently, in 2017, he's 98 years old, bent like the twisted trunk of an aged cedar tree and deaf as that same cedar post.

However, his mind is as sharp as some of the Deep Creek mountain pinnacles, and especially, his memory of long ago is as crystal blue clear as his eyes. He lives, for the most part, independently, a good two stone throws from my house. His double-wide trailer home sets on a hill overlooking the Arthur Kelley place where he says he spent the best years of his life. On my daily walk to spend time with him, I conceal my note pad and pen in the inside breast pocket of my chore coat. I sit near in the rocking chair. After a time, I begin by saying, "Tell me about..." He points his old crooked finger, his blue eyes get that far-off look, and he starts. As inconspicuously as possible, I write. The hours quickly pass as he and I become temporarily lost in adventures of long ago. I rush home with my pocket full of treasures and begin to word process. To say the least, his stories are usually lively. They are filled with old-timed cowboy wit and wisdom, but they also, sometimes, contain an off-color ending that may leave the reader shaking his or her head in consternation.

He has adamantly refused to be recorded or quoted. He stubbornly tells people, "I don't want somebody writing my stories down 'cause I don't always tell the truth!" Obviously, I never followed instructions very well.

What follows are the musings and meanderings of an antique cowboy, who has lived a tough, long, and remarkably unbelievable life. These memoirs are inklings into some of the souls—human, equine, bovine, and canine alike—that he has met along the way. So the disclaimer to the reader is this: laugh, cry, feel free to be a skeptic, believe what you will, and enjoy the memories.

The first entry in the tattered notebook dated February 1, 1993, reads as follows:

> *Jay Hicks said about his wife, Leatha, as she was putting on a pair of long-handled underwear that belonged to him (Jay was a slight built man weighing maybe 125 pounds soaking wet, and his wife probably outweighed him doubly), "Chreeest,\* they stretched out and looked just like chicken wire!"*

For whatever reason possessed me to start writing with that particular tidbit, I'll never know. But I was hooked and have been jotting them down ever since.

\*Jay Hicks' alternative explicative for taking the Lord's name in vain.

# Some of the Brands
## Used in the Deep Creek Country

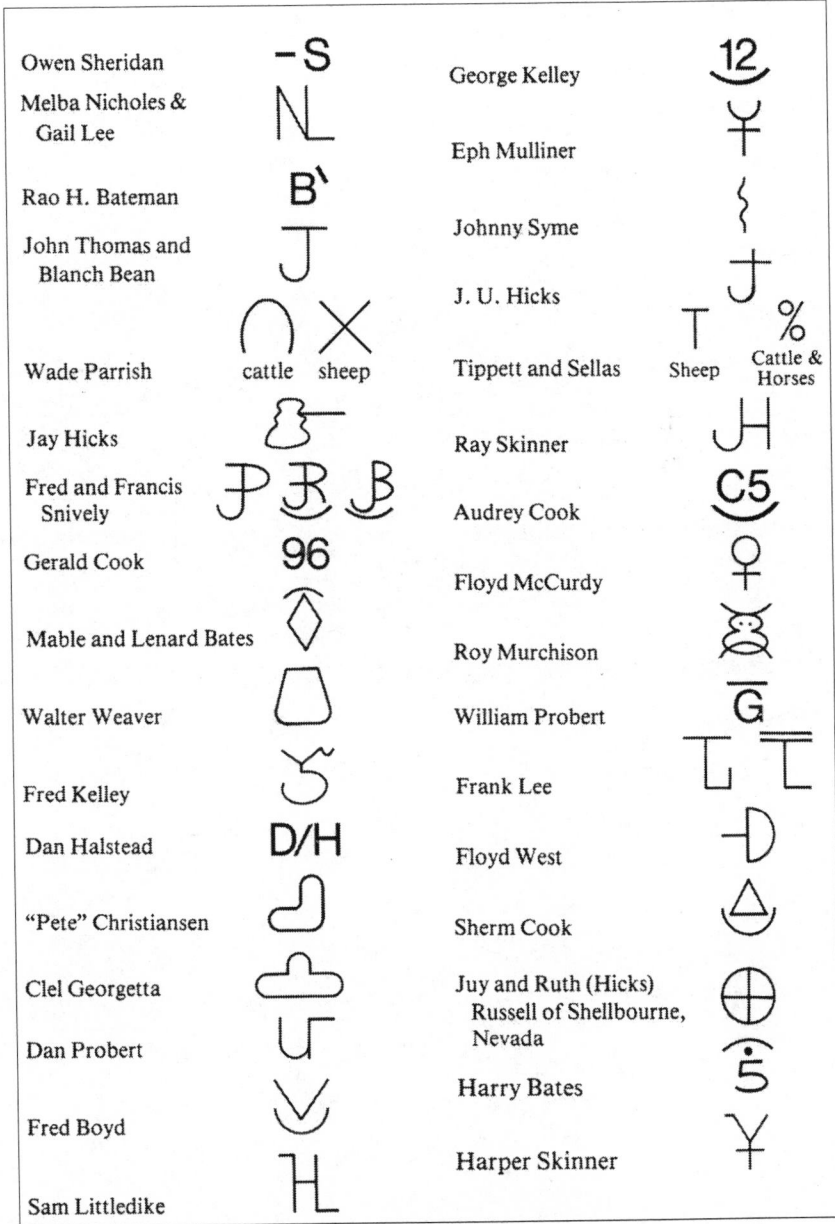

| | |
|---|---|
| Owen Sheridan | George Kelley |
| Melba Nicholes & Gail Lee | |
| | Eph Mulliner |
| Rao H. Bateman | |
| John Thomas and Blanch Bean | Johnny Syme |
| | J. U. Hicks |
| Wade Parrish    cattle    sheep | Tippett and Sellas    Sheep    Cattle & Horses |
| Jay Hicks | Ray Skinner |
| Fred and Francis Snively | Audrey Cook |
| Gerald Cook | Floyd McCurdy |
| Mable and Lenard Bates | Roy Murchison |
| Walter Weaver | William Probert |
| Fred Kelley | Frank Lee |
| Dan Halstead | Floyd West |
| "Pete" Christiansen | Sherm Cook |
| Clel Georgetta | Juy and Ruth (Hicks) Russell of Shellbourne, Nevada |
| Dan Probert | Harry Bates |
| Fred Boyd | Harper Skinner |
| Sam Littledike | |

*Courtesy Ron Bateman,* **Deep Creek Reflections.** *1984.*

# Partial Genealogy of Gerald Worlton Cook

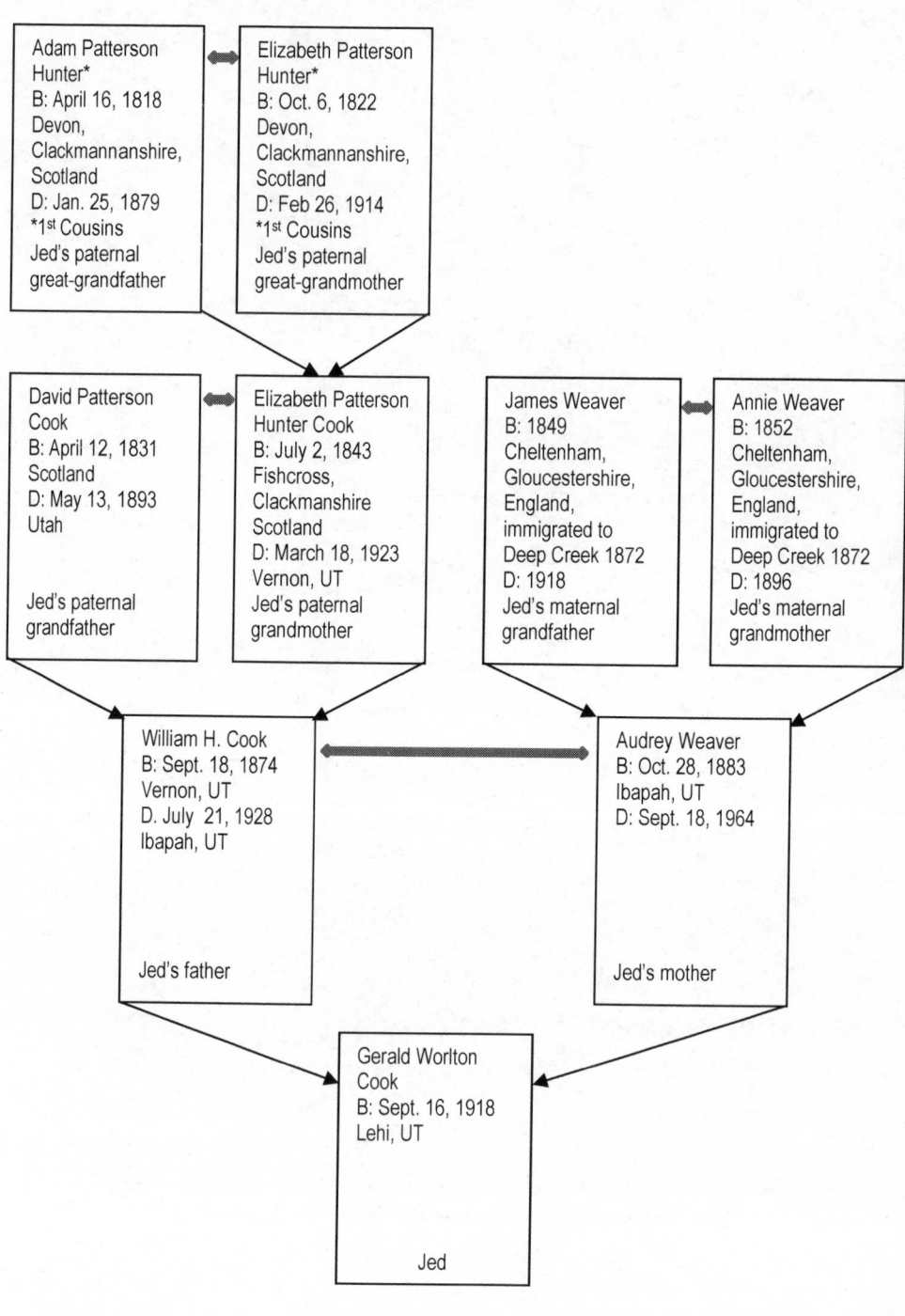

Adam Patterson Hunter*
B: April 16, 1818
Devon, Clackmannanshire, Scotland
D: Jan. 25, 1879
*1st Cousins
Jed's paternal great-grandfather

Elizabeth Patterson Hunter*
B: Oct. 6, 1822
Devon, Clackmannanshire, Scotland
D: Feb 26, 1914
*1st Cousins
Jed's paternal great-grandmother

David Patterson Cook
B: April 12, 1831
Scotland
D: May 13, 1893
Utah

Jed's paternal grandfather

Elizabeth Patterson Hunter Cook
B: July 2, 1843
Fishcross, Clackmanshire Scotland
D: March 18, 1923
Vernon, UT
Jed's paternal grandmother

James Weaver
B: 1849
Cheltenham, Gloucestershire, England, immigrated to Deep Creek 1872
D: 1918
Jed's maternal grandfather

Annie Weaver
B: 1852
Cheltenham, Gloucestershire, England, immigrated to Deep Creek 1872
D: 1896
Jed's maternal grandmother

William H. Cook
B: Sept. 18, 1874
Vernon, UT
D. July 21, 1928
Ibapah, UT

Jed's father

Audrey Weaver
B: Oct. 28, 1883
Ibapah, UT
D: Sept. 18, 1964

Jed's mother

Gerald Worlton Cook
B: Sept. 16, 1918
Lehi, UT

Jed

# Timeline

# Elizabeth Patterson Hunter

My great-grandmother Hunter came to the United States from Scotland. The ship she was on traveled around Florida, up the Gulf of Mexico, and onto the Mississippi River. Hunters and Cooks come together on that boat. They left from St. Louis, Missouri, and come across the plains with Brigham Young and his group. They traveled by ox cart. She couldn't ride in the wagon because it was too rough, and she was pregnant.

On the trail, she had twins under the shelter of the wagon box. It was the middle of winter. People heated rocks to keep her and the twin girls warm. She had a big family. One of her daughters, Elizabeth, married David Patterson Cook, and they homesteaded a ranch in Vernon, Utah. They also had a big family of 13 kids. I'm related to half the Cooks, Rydalchs, Durfees, and Williams around Tooele County. Their mothers were my aunts, and the Cook families' fathers were my uncles.

*Elizabeth Patterson Hunter in her Scottish regalia. Circa 1870.*

# Cook Boys Arrive in Deep Creek

Charlie Herron, who later married Nina Felt, worked for a sheep outfit that traveled around. The year was 1898. He happened to run into the Cook boys, who lived in Vernon, Utah, at that time. My uncles Abe, Adam, and Johnny, and my father Will Cook came to Deep Creek after hearing about it from Charlie Herron. Adam went back to Vernon, but the other three settled in the area. Abe married Evelyn Weaver. Will married Audrey Weaver. Johnny married Edna Brown (Old Lady Snively's daughter).

Fred Boyd told me the story of the first time he met the Cook boys. He was just a kid, and his mother and he lived in Callao. They had come to Devine's store for groceries and were on the way home with the team and wagon. They were headed down Overland Canyon. They saw a string of riders coming up the canyon. It was Charlie Herron and the four Cook boys. They all had musical instruments tied on their saddles. Will had a bass fiddle tied on the horn and a guitar case tied behind the saddle. He was riding a little mustang horse. Adam and Abe had their fiddles, and Johnny had his banjo. Mrs. Boyd fixed everyone sandwiches to eat, and afterwards they played their instruments. Fred said it was the prettiest music he ever heard.

# Ibapah Major Ranches

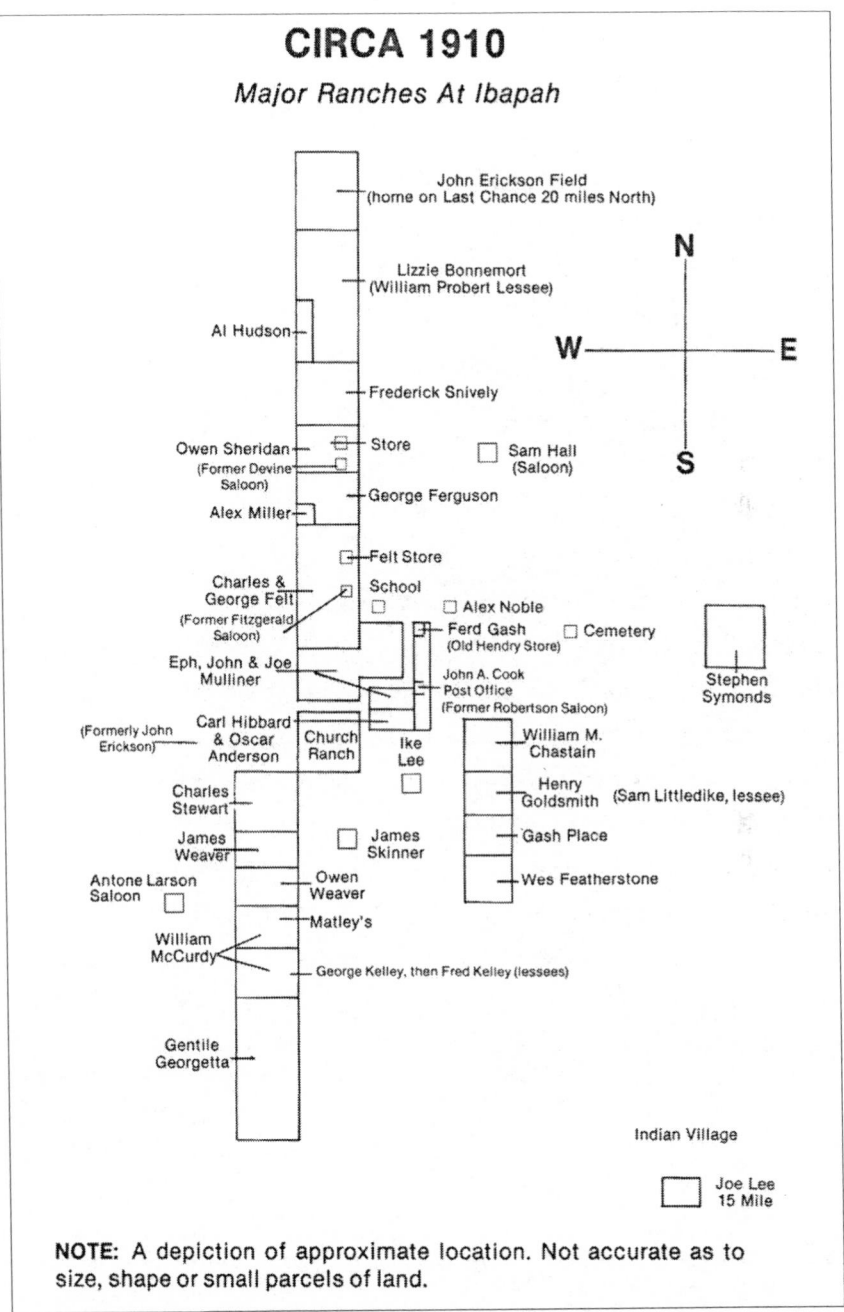

*Courtesy Ron Bateman,* **Deep Creek Reflections.** *1984.*

3

# Ibapah Settlement

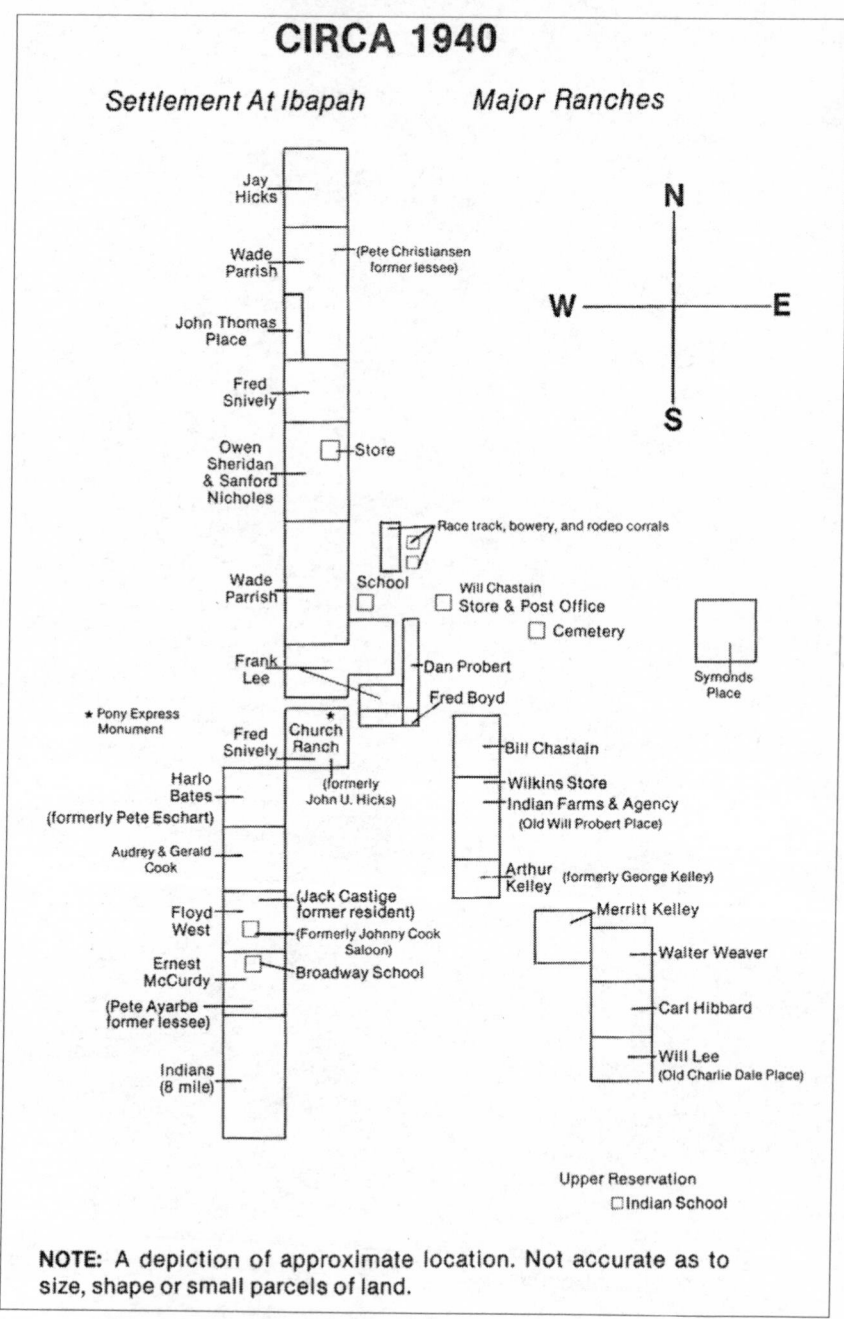

**CIRCA 1940**

Settlement At Ibapah          Major Ranches

Jay Hicks

Wade Parrish — (Pete Christiansen former lessee)

John Thomas Place

Fred Snively

Owen Sheridan & Sanford Nicholes — Store

Race track, bowery, and rodeo corrals

Wade Parrish — School

Will Chastain Store & Post Office

Cemetery

Symonds Place

Frank Lee — Dan Probert

Fred Boyd

★ Pony Express Monument

Fred Snively — ★ Church Ranch (formerly John U. Hicks)

Bill Chastain

Harlo Bates (formerly Pete Eschart)

Wilkins Store

Indian Farms & Agency (Old Will Probert Place)

Audrey & Gerald Cook

Arthur Kelley (formerly George Kelley)

Floyd West — (Jack Castige former resident)

(Formerly Johnny Cook Saloon)

Merritt Kelley

Ernest McCurdy — Broadway School

Walter Weaver

(Pete Ayarbe former lessee)

Carl Hibbard

Will Lee (Old Charlie Dale Place)

Indians (8 mile)

Upper Reservation
☐ Indian School

**NOTE:** A depiction of approximate location. Not accurate as to size, shape or small parcels of land.

*Courtesy Ron Bateman,* **Deep Creek Reflections.** *1984.*

# Ibapah Creeks and Canyons

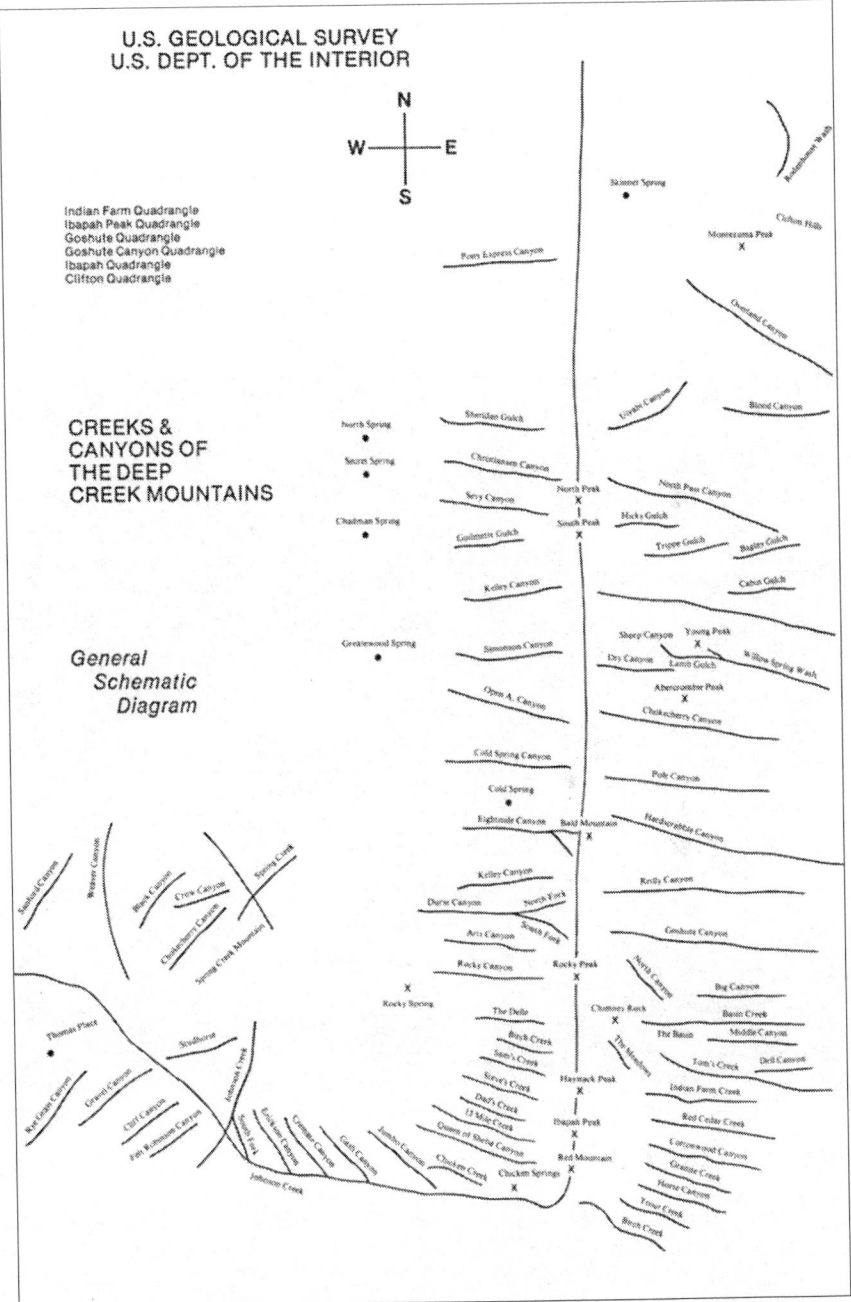

*Courtesy Ron Bateman,* **Deep Creek Reflections.** *1984.*

# Early Years

I, Gerald Worlton Cook, was born to William and Audrey Weaver Cook on September 16, 1918. When folks ask me if I've lived in Deep Creek all my life I say, "No, I lived in Lehi, Utah, until I had my first bowel movement. Then my parents moved me to Deep Creek, and I've been here ever since."

My folks took up the 160-acre place my granddad Jim Weaver homesteaded on the west side of Deep Creek valley.

*William, Audrey, Leslie, and Mary Cook. Circa 1912.*

A horse reared over on my dad and smashed his hip. He supposedly developed tuberculosis of the hip, and in later years it went to his lungs. My parents, Will and Audrey, and my family spent summers at the Queen of Sheba mine on the southern end of the Deep Creek Mountain range. We lived there on doctor's orders because the fresh air was supposed to be good for my dad's lungs. When I was a little boy, I remember following old Charlie Dale around as he fished and hunted sage chickens. I remember people being afraid because of the TB, but Floyd and Blanche West weren't afraid, and neither was Lyle Hibbard. I remember my dad going down to the corral if visitors came, especially little kids. I think now that he never had TB at all and probably died of emphysema. He smoked until the day he died.

In 1923, my dad was in the Ely hospital with blood poisoning. A man from Ely by the name of Archibald took my mother and me over Schellbourne Pass to Ely to visit Dad on Christmas. Mr. Archibald had a Model T. We had a blanket wrapped around our feet and legs to keep warm. The blanket caught on fire. Mr. Archibald stopped the car, put out the fire, and threw the blanket away.

*Will Cook (left), Gerald Cook (front), Audrey Cook with LeRoy Littledyke, Mary Cook Littledyke, Alma (Al) Littledyke. 1927.*

On this trip, I remember my mother telling me of her little brother. He had gotten kicked in the head with a horse. Her dad hitched the team and wagon, and they headed for Ely, some 90 miles west. When they got on top of Schellbourne Pass, the little boy died. There was nothing to do for him, so they turned around and went back to Deep Creek.

*Will and Audrey Cook ranch. Circa 1930.*

When Fred Boyd was a little boy, he lived with Charlie Stewart and his wife. They lived where the Bates ranch is today. Charlie went down the valley after the mail and didn't come home, so Mrs. Stewart sent Fred down the valley to find him. It was winter, and Fred came by the Probert place. At that time, Uncle Johnny Cook owned it and had a saloon there. That's where Fred found Charlie and Will. They had been at the saloon for a good while. They were pretty well lit. My dad was on a bronc, and Charlie was holding the snubbing rope. It was actually two lasso ropes tied together. They'd run out to the edge of the meadow covered with ice. My dad would holler, "Pop the whip, Charlie! Pop the whip!"

Charlie would let go of the rope, and my dad, atop his horse, would shoot out over the ice, the horse spraddled out. It's a wonder that horse never fell down.

My dad was full of hell. One time him and Uncle Carl Hibbard were headed to a dance. They'd been partying. My dad was driving the team and buggy. Uncle Carl hollered, "Throw the lines away, Will!"

So my dad let go of the reins. When he did, those horses ran like a bat out of hell. When they turned the corner there in the lane by John Mulner's place, the horses ran off into the fence. They busted up the buggy pretty good, but they were all right.

My dad was crippled and couldn't ride, so he drove the buggy around the sheep herd in a buggy and team. Sometimes I'd go with him, and I remember him kidding me. It tickled me so much I nearly fell out of the buggy, but he grabbed me at the last minute and pulled me back in.

I remember my dad driving around our herd of sheep and seeing an old ewe having a lamb. I wondered how in the hell did that lamb get there?

I seen my grandmother Elizabeth Hunter Cook only one time. My dad told me this story. One winter my Uncle John, who lived in Gold Hill, got very sick with pneumonia. People thought he was going to die. My grandmother boarded the Western Pacific train in Burmester, Utah, to come see Uncle John. My dad drove the buggy to Wendover to pick her up. She was the first woman to ride the Western Pacific train from Grantsville to Wendover. The year was 1910.

When my grandmother Cook died in Vernon, Utah, the family sent word by telegram to Mr. Lord in Gold Hill, who ran the telegraph office. My dad never got the message until two weeks after she was dead and buried. I remember my dad put his head in his hands and cried like a baby when he got the news.

There was a man named John Winsell, who went by the name of Dutch John. He was a Swede from the old country. He spoke broken English. He herded sheep for my dad and worked around the valley. As a little boy, I recall Dutch John crawling into a hole under the house, and when he tried to back out, the sheepskin coat he was wearing came up around his head, and he was stuck. My dad got a hold of his heels and pulled him out. When he was all the way out, he produced arms full of pups. Some things just stick with you. I was about five years old.

Dutch John worked for Georgetta on the Eight-Mile Ranch for a time. For some reason Mr. Georgetta didn't pay him, so he took a mule in payment. Dutch John went to work for McCurdys in Chin Creek. Georgetta sent him a letter demanding the mule be returned.

Dutch John said, "I take a piece of brown paper off the bacon, and I write: 'Dear Mr. Etta,'... I scratch out the Dear... 'Mr. Etta, you son-of-a-bitch, I don't know if I'll see you before, but I'll see you in hell, and that's where I'll deliver the mule!'"

Deep Creek folks held dances for many occasions. Mrs. Sheridan held a New Year's Dance and a Halloween Masquerade Ball. There were wedding dances too. People would load the wagon, harness the team, bundle up under blankets, and go down the valley. Uncle Abe, my dad, my brother Les, and my sister Mary all played for the dances. When I grew older, I played the accordion for dances too.

Milt Hibbard had a push-button accordion that you played like a mouth organ by pushing and pulling on it. It never had no keys. I taught myself how to play on that. I never learned to read music, but I've played the accordion all my life.

I remember my dad taking his pocket knife out and sliding it along the strings to play his guitar like a steel guitar and my sister Mary singing.

When I was just a kid, I remember going to all-night dances in Deep Creek. Gold Hill was a boom town then. The guys would come down from Gold Hill and get drunk and fight.

Sherm and Beth Cook lived in a cabin in Spring Valley up Munsey Creek. Sherm was working in a mine there. Glen was a little kid. They left him alone, hitched the team and wagon, and traveled over here to a dance some forty miles east. Oh, there was an old guy down the canyon that would "watch" Glen.

Sherm was outside of the schoolhouse having a drink. He said, "Shit," within earshot of Stan Kearney's girlfriend. It made Stan mad, and he hit Sherm and knocked him out. My dad and Uncle Carl Hibbard thought it was kind of a dirty trick to knock Sherm out like that. They jumped right into the fight, and they were standing their own. I guess they straightened the other guys out pretty good too.

*4th of July Rodeo and Horse Race at the Bowery corral. Circa 1930.*

People had picnics, 4th of July celebrations, and rodeos at the Bowery. The bronc riders of high esteem in my eyes were Lyle Hibbard, Sam Littledyke, Archie Hall, Gus Dugan, and Jimmy

11

Steele. On one 4th of July day, Jimmy rode Les' mule with only a rope around his middle. Jimmy was about 15 years old at the time. You talk about buck! Jimmy had a big hat, and boy, could he ride. Old Man Parker in the audience said to his wife, "Oh, Mama, did you see that boy ride that mule… And did you hear that mule fart?"

*Gerald and his sister Mary. Circa 1923.*

When I was a little boy, Orvil Ferguson lived in our field in a sheep camp. He trapped coyotes around the valley and had a little herd of sheep. He came to my mother's house one time when me and Les had the mumps. Our faces were all swelled up. He came in, but he never sat down. He just stood by the door. He kept looking at us. He finally said to my mother, "Maybe I better go, Audrey."

I remember her saying to him, "You might as well stay now, Orvil; you're already exposed."

He never did get the mumps.

Orvil used to walk real straight. He rode his horses the same way, with his back so straight and his chest puffed out. He knew how to sit a horse.

# School Days

I rode horseback from the Cook place up to Broadway School starting in the first grade. Broadway School was north of Eudeene Parker's ranch. Ray Skinner later moved it to where it sits today and added onto and remodeled it. Eudeene Parker lives there now. Bill West, Glen Rice, and I started school together. Margaret Reed from Lund was our teacher. In second grade, Erma Faucett from Ely was our teacher. Glen's father Jack brought a quirt to school for the teacher to tame Glen. (A quirt is a braided rawhide whip used on horses and backsides.) Glen would get so nervous he'd have to sneak out to the outside toilet to have a smoke.

*Helen Kelley (Fred Kelley's daughter) and Jed.*
*Helen was in the 8th grade when Jed started school at Broadway.*
*Notice Audrey's turkeys in the background. 1924.*

Glen Rice was a tough little scrapper, and he liked to fight. His hands were so damn rough and chapped, when he hit you, it felt like coarse sandpaper on your face. We were good friends, but it sure hurt when his sandpaper fist would glance off my nose.

I had a dog that liked to fight too. I got that black and white shepherd pup from Jack Rice. I called him Bob. In the winter, I'd hook him up to my sleigh on the hill where the road had packed-down snow. He hooked up with just a breast collar. He hated Floyd West's dog. I'd holler, "Get him, Bob!" and off we'd go like a bat out of hell. When we got to West's place, he'd back out of that collar and run West's dog up on the porch and tear into him. Blanche West would come out of the house and beat them apart with a broom. Bob knew he was in trouble, so he'd get back in the collar, and he'd take me home.

A car went down the road one day when Bob and I were sitting on the hill with the sleigh. A dog stuck his head out of the back window. Bob chased that car, trying to get at the other dog, clear down to the end of the lane, a good two miles. He finally turned around and pulled me home.

When that dog got old, he was so stiff in the shoulders he couldn't go—too much pulling me in the sleigh and fighting.

Jack Rice was a teamster and a good one. He and his family lived in a dugout shack under the hill there on the west side of the valley. I would often stand out beside the road on the top of the hill at my mother's place and watch for Jack. One muddy winter day, here come Jack and his team. He hauled freight and had four horses, or sometimes six or eight, on the front. Jack would call a horse by name, and that horse would pull and make the mud fly going up that slimy hill. I asked Jack how he trained them to know their names like that. Jack said he had tacks rigged in the cinch, and when he called out their name, he pulled on their cinch at the same time.

14

# My Sister Mildred

My parent's oldest child was a girl. Her name was Mildred. She was two years old when she contracted spinal meningitis and died. My dad wasn't home. He was hauling freight to Toana. When he came home and my mother started to tell him, he said he already knew. He had saw her, and later, as he lay dying, he saw her hand reaching out to him again.

*Mildred Cook.*
*Born November 6, 1901. Died January 5, 1903.*

# My Dad's Deathbed

My father Will had tuberculosis and died when I was nine years old. Uncle Abe and the rest of the family were all there at the old Cook place, as my dad was very ill. He got worse in the middle of the night. He knew he was dying. At sunup, they woke me and asked me to come to my father's bedside. Dad had waited until morning to talk to me. He took my hand in his and told me, "Don't smoke, don't drink, be kind to others, and above all, be honest." Then he gave me his watch.

He looked up at his brother, Abe, and asked, "What do I do now, Abe?"

Uncle Abe replied, "Give 'er up, Will. Give 'er up." Ten minutes later he was gone.

*William Cook's final resting place. Deep Creek Cemetery.*
*July 21, 1928.*

I penned a letter titled, *My Most Prized Possession*. The following are my exact words:

*My most cherished thing was given to me when I was a kid. A watch given to me by my dad on his death bed just minutes before he died. The watch was given to him by Happy Jack.*

*It was in a big silver closed-in case and I took it into Lehi, Utah, to an old jeweler. The name was Sorenson's Jewelers. Sorenson put it in a gold case. It was a pretty watch, engraved with an elk on the back, 24-jeweled Elgin, the winding stem comes out the side of the number three.*

*Years ago, my folks had to go to a railroad station at northern Nevada called Toana for supplies. It took a week round-trip with horses and wagon. They camped along the road. They camped at the old Johnson ranch, which is half-way between Wendover and Wells. It was a cold fall day. There was a water tank there about eight feet across and 10 feet high. Dad got up on the ladder, reached down with a bucket to get some water, and his watch fell out of his bib overalls pocket into the water. Dad took his clothes off, dove down to the bottom of that frigid water, and got his watch. I was nine years old when Dad took my hand and gave me the watch. I am 88 years old, and I still remember that morning as if it was yesterday.*

After my dad died, my brother Les wore the watch, too. One time the watch worked its way out of Les' pocket when he was up in the South Mountains herding sheep. When he saw he had lost it, he and I went back over our tracks and finally found it laying in some leaves under a quaking aspen tree.

I still have the watch. It is over 100 years old. Some time back, I took it into a jeweler in Salt Lake. He said that the time piece had worn out, and it would cost more to get it fixed than it was probably worth. It sits in my drawer now.

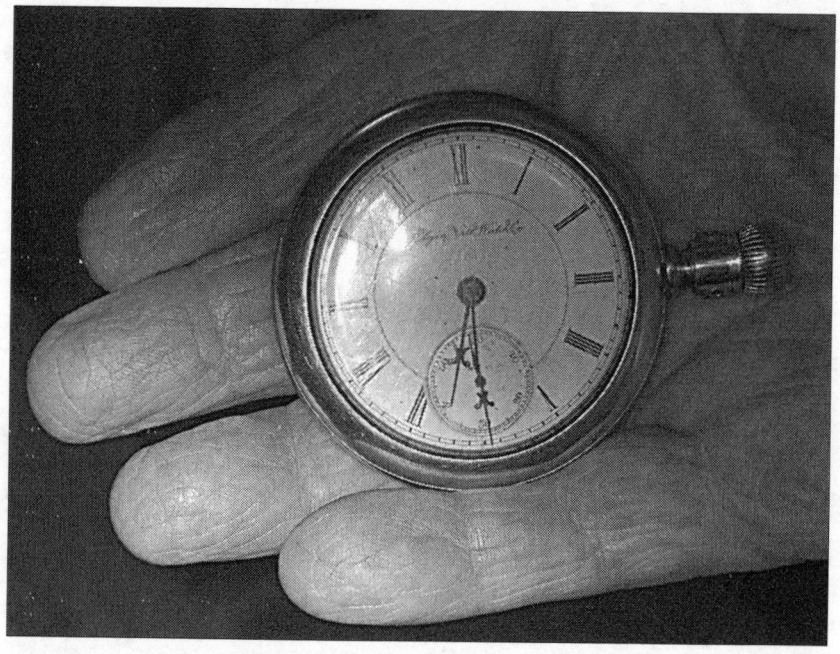

*Jed's watch.*

# School Down the Valley

After my father died, it was decided that I'd go down the valley to school. There were two rooms and two teachers. My first teacher there was Carol Madsen. Everybody rode horses to school. The Hibbard kids rode from the Hibbard place, seven or eight miles away. The Christiansen kids rode from Bonnemonts' place, up through the field to school. Jaceways rode from the Ferguson place, the lone house still standing in Knight's pasture. Elma Kelley rode from Kelley Spring. She had an over-grown slicker coat that belonged to her dad. Us kids would stand out on the steps of the school house. We'd see her run old Danger as hard as he could come, with that slicker flying out over his behind.

We tied our horses to the Bowery corrals while we attended school. One morning when Danger was tied to the Bowery corral, a crazed mare came whinnying up the valley. She ran to old Danger and started kicking him. The mare fell down and couldn't get up. She had a bite on her leg. There was a report of rabid dogs running around, and supposedly, one of them had bitten her. Fred Boyd took a gun and shot the mare.

My cousins, the Beels, lived on part of the old Cook place in a log cabin down by the corrals. I'd pick up Jay, who was my age, and his little sister Ethyl, with the horse and buggy, and we'd go to school. One time when we hit the west end of the lane, we decided to go a little faster. Jay poked old Ted in the butt with a stick. He was running as hard as he could when we turned John Mulner's corner. Two wheels went off in the creek, and two wheels stayed on the bridge. The buggy went in the air. I dropped the lines, and the horse ran into some of Mr. Mulner's machinery, where it stopped the horse. John Mulner was out to the corral doing his morning chores. I can see him coming yet. He jumped the fence and grabbed me by the arm. He said, "You go ahead and kill yourself, but get that little girl out of there!"

I was scared of John Mulner for a long while after that. I'd duck my head when I went through the lane on my way to school.

Ibapah School House, Erected In 1904, Ibapah, Utah

*Ibapah School House. Down the valley.*

John Mulner's brother Tom cussed me out for riding too fast, too. He'd say, "You little bugger, you're riding that mare too damn fast. If you don't quit, I'm gonna kick your damn A double S!"

He'd tell me, "You little bugger, you're gonna get rheumatism from the sweat on that horse's back." I didn't have a saddle so I rode bareback to school. One time he gave me a horsehair pad that he had made to cushion my backside.

In the sixth grade, Gene Christiansen and I skipped school for a week or so to chase mustangs. Gene threatened his little brother and sister with a beating if they told. We'd sneak out through the west end of the lane and chase the mustangs when they came into drink at Mary's Hole. When it came time to go home, Gene'd ride back of the meadow to his house, and I'd ride west to my mother's place. I thought I had gotten away with it, until mother got a note to meet with the teacher. She went down to school, and Mr. Rogers said he hadn't seen her son Gerald in school for a week.

For our punishment, the teacher took out a bunch of papers and a pencil. He had us write, "I like to sluff school, I like to sluff school, I like to sluff school," over and over again. We missed recess, after recess, after recess, filling those papers up. I thought we never would get done writing.

# Mr. Rogers

Oaf Rogers was the teacher. When you went in the school building, you could hear the clock on the wall ticking. It was that quiet. He was strict now, and you knew you better be quiet and work. But when you went outside, it was pretty wild. Mr. Rogers would put the boxing gloves on and box with us kids. He didn't mind knocking you down. He was pretty handy with his mitts.

Back then, a lot of us kids around here played a mouth organ. Newell Kelley, Kenny Snively, Earl Jaceway, and me all played. On one occasion, Oaf Rogers called us in to play. We got up on the old music stand in the school house. Leatha Weaver could chord on the piano. She accompanied us. Mr. Rogers laughed and slapped his knee. It tickled the hell out of him.

In the 9th grade, we were on our own. The teacher helped us, but we did our work independently. There was Dan Lee, Jay Beel, Marion Kelley, Earl Jaceway, and me. We had gathered up some horses around the valley, so when we got our school work done, we had a couple of rodeos on our free time. One day Mr. Rogers called us in and told us we better quit. He hated to tell us, but he had to put a stop to it. He said, "I enjoy watching you, but I can't keep the other kids in their desks. I'm just afraid somebody will get hurt."

I always liked Mr. Rogers and had a great deal of respect for him. In later years, after Joyce and I were married, we attended a rodeo in Delta and went on down to Kanosh to visit Mr. Rogers. He had a farm there and was out in the field. It tickled the hell out of him for us to come and visit.

I went to Tooele in the 9th grade for a short time. Doyle Lymans, Oren Probert, and I went to stay with the Droubays. The house still stands on Utah Avenue where we boarded. Doyle and Oren were cousins. Their mothers, Millie and May, were sisters. Doyle and I didn't stay long. In fact, we'd show up for roll call at school, and then we'd skip out. That was the end of my formal education.

When we decided to come home, we caught a ride to Grantsville, and then we thumbed a ride to Wendover. I stayed with Doyle's folks, Ace and Millie Lymans, until I could get a ride back to Deep Creek. Times were hard. Millie took in laundry from the whores who worked at the Blue Goose. One day, she sent Doyle and me up to get the laundry. We was so scared those whores would get us that we came back to the Lyman's house without the laundry.

# Herding Sheep

My earliest recollection of helping take care of sheep happened when I was 10 or 11 years old, after my dad had died. A Basque sheepherder named Mike Izaki leased 1,200-1,500 head of sheep from Steve Doutre in Spring Valley. He kept them in the meadows at the McCurdy place west of my mother's ranch. I helped him lamb them and keep them together. After we got the sheep settled, Mike would cook up pork and beans, peas, and eggs together. It sure tasted good.

My mother would get me out of bed early in the morning to go help. The sheep would drift out of the meadow in the mornings, and I'd bring them back so the coyotes didn't get the lambs. They'd shade up in the day, but straggle out to the west hills in the evening, and I'd get on my horse and push them back into the meadow. Mike went to Ely for a week, and I took care of the sheep by myself then.

Old Man McCurdy (William) lived in a cabin on the McCurdy place. He was 100 years old and still taking care of himself. He was a Civil War veteran. I'd go visit with him. He was a good cook and made good pies. I'd get right down by his ear and holler to make him hear me. He'd say, "By George, you'll have to speak up a little." He said he lost his hearing from standing too close to the big guns during the war. My mother would make butter and give him the buttermilk. He'd say, "By George, better than beer!"

Wade Parrish and Floyd West had large herds of sheep in the South Mountains. My brother Les herded sheep for Floyd and Wade. Wade came to Deep Creek before Floyd. He had a large herd of sheep for as long as I can remember. Floyd also had large herds of sheep. He leased the reservation from the Goshute Indian tribe. Leo Pete kept the upper herd of about 1,500 head in Johnson

24

Canyon. Tommy Wash took care of 1,500 head on the north end of the reservation. My brother Les helped both sheepherders and camped at the Queen of Sheba. During the depression, Floyd went bankrupt and lost his big herd of sheep.

*L to R: Unknown with dog, Charles Felt, Floyd West, Blanche Felt West, Chloe Felt Parrish, and Wade Parrish. Circa 1915.*

*Basin Sheep Camp. Wade, Phyllis, and Joyce Parrish, and Thelma Lee. Circa 1937.*

Wade Parrish was Floyd West's uncle. They both came from North Carolina. They originally had a big herd of sheep together, but later went their separate ways. Wade lived up to the West place in a big adobe home in the meadow for a time.

One 4th of July, my mother and I took off for the South Mountains to spend it with Les. We stayed for three or four days, and when it came time to come home, I was torn as to where I wanted to be. We got down in the flat. I decided I would go back with Les. I untied my horse from the wagon and rode back towards the hills. I got to the sheep camp at dark, as Les was going around the sheep. Les looked up and said, "Do you know what you do want?" I bawled like a baby. I was 10 or 12 years old.

Wade Parrish, my future father-in-law, was always good to me. He got eggs from my mother. He'd take a case of eggs and maybe some butter or cream to sheep camp. Wade would stop and pick me up, and we'd go to Gravel where he had a herd of sheep. Sage chickens would come into the spring behind the cabin to get a drink. We'd always have sage chicken to eat. I was always riding a damn horse. Wade would jump me for a trade and throw in some money to boot. I know he did that just 'cause I didn't have no dad.

I worked a lot for Wade Parrish. I traded horses with him too. Whenever he needed help with cows, he would call on me or Dan Lee. Dan lived with his family in a cabin across the way, where the Bowery corrals were.

After my dad died, my mother and I used to harness our horse and buggy and go to visit Uncle Carl and Aunt Vinnie Hibbard through Round Valley, on an old bumpy road. It was quite a trip from the west side to the east side of the valley, eight miles or so. We'd go on special occasions like the 4th of July. I was just a kid. It felt like I was going to New York.

*Sheep crowded in the shearing corral. Circa 1935.*

*A little Goshute girl playing on the wool sacks. Circa 1935.*

On one occasion, my mother and I were driving a herd of sheep to put with other ranchers' sheep up on Bald Mountain. The day was hot, and the sheep didn't want to move. I sassed my mother, and she took after me on her horse. I was riding a little mustang, and she was riding a bigger mare that we worked and rode both. Her horse was faster. She caught up with me and slapped me on the back with her reins. I never sassed my mother after that.

*Shearing time. Joyce Parrish pictured third from left. Circa 1935.*

*Shearing time. Circa 1935.*

Everybody used to get together to shear the herds of sheep. Teepees were all around the shearing grounds. There was 3,000 or so head of sheep to be sheared. The Indians sheared the sheep and stayed until the shearing of the wool was done. They done all the work with hand shears until, later on, some outfit came in with electric shears and did the job.

*Loading the wool sacks on the trucks. Circa 1935.*

Badger Tom was one of the main shearers and sheepherders. He and his family went around the valley with a team and wagon. His daughter Maxine Tom had a pretty little palomino mare. The mare would sometimes be tied behind the wagon, or Maxine would be riding her. She let us kids ride her pretty horse once in a while.

The prettiest sight I ever saw was when I was riding my horse across the reservation on my way to sheep camp. Leo Pete's sister Mary was standing in a window of a log cabin as I rode by, and the wood boards framed her just like a picture.

One summer, when I was herding sheep with Les in Johnson Canyon, it rained and rained. Leo Pete was taking care of Floyd's upper herd of about 1,500 head of sheep. They had gotten mixed with Henriod's herd of sheep from Pleasant Valley. We corralled them and separated them in the downpour. Afterwards, Leo's wife had dinner waiting for us in the Dutch oven. We went in the teepee out of the rain. There was a baby in a cradleboard. We were thankful to eat and get dried off.

*Leslie Cook on Brownie. Circa 1936.*

Les was camped up at the Queen, so when it appeared the weather had cleared, we started back for camp. There was a trail that went from Johnson Canyon to the Queen. The fog rolled in, and we got lost. The fog was so thick I couldn't see my hand. We stopped. Les got some logs, dug around a tree, and built a fire. When the fog lifted, we could see we were in the head of Erickson Canyon. I remember looking down when the fog cleared, and it looked like the whole world spread out before me down below.

Les played a violin. Oftentimes Tommy Pete, Leo Pete's brother, would come up to his camp at the Queen of Sheba. Tommy played a violin, too. They played together and used to make some beautiful music and have a lot of fun.

When Les herded sheep for Wade Parrish up in the Basin, Tom and Frank Bishop helped him.

Les was a good cook. He used to cook "dough god" (sheepherder bread) in a Dutch oven at sheep camp. When it was cooked, he'd turn it over onto the table in the sheep camp. You'd break it off in pieces, and what you didn't eat, the dog got. Sheepherder bread and a mutton chop is the best damn meal anybody could want.

*Wade and Chloe Parrish headed to sheep camp. Circa 1930.*

When I was 14 years old, I had a sheep camp and herded 250 head of sheep in Round Valley. One day Newell Kelley showed up, and I invited him to eat. Newell wanted to know what was in the can. He tasted peanut butter for the first time and darn near ate the whole thing.

One time, my cousin Sherm Cook and my brother were herding sheep for Wade Parrish. Their dog chased out a bobcat. The cat was scared of the dog, and having no place else to run, it jumped up behind the saddle with Les! Its claws were digging in, and the horse was pitching and kicking up, but the bobcat paid no attention, as it was looking down at the dog.

# Midget

The year was around 1928 or '29. Sherm Cook was working for Clel Georgetta on the eight-mile side of the valley. Sherm liked to chase mustangs. They used to come into drink on Spring Creek. We chased them off the water one day, and a little brown colt with a star on her forehead was left behind. She was probably only a week or so old. She followed Sherm's horse down to my brother Les' Model T Ford. She didn't have a rope or anything on her. We put her in the back seat of the Model T and brought her home. I raised her on a bucket. When she grew up, I rode her for a long time. I rode her to school. Midget was her name.

One day, Bill West and I were going up to Sanford to visit my sister and her husband. Some mustangs came out of the creek, and I took after them on my good mustang mare. Then we went onto Sanford. It was a good 15 miles. When we returned to the home ranch that same day, some more mustangs ran out from the creek. I chased them too. It was a hot day. She stiffened up—I guess I melted her. I left her by the gate at Georgetta's place. When I came back the next morning, she was dead. I cried. Old Man Georgetta cussed me out. He said to me, "Now see what you done! You satisfied now?" I never will forget it.

# Georgetta's Flood

Old Man Georgetta was a miner before he got Eight-Mile Ranch. He had saved some pretty good money. He hired a carpenter and built a nice two-story home on the place. The carpenter built a fancy four-hole shit house. One spring, the creek overflowed its banks. There was water everywhere. My mother and I seen that shit house come floating by, sitting up straight, just like a boat. Boards and other junk would go floating by too, and every once in a while, a chicken or two would be riding on a board or log. The shit house got high-centered on a knoll where the road turns into Bate's ranch. After the flood was through, Georgettas come and hauled it back home.

# Bimbo

When I was about 15 years old, Sammy Littledyke sold some horses to the Cleveland ranch at the south end of Spring Valley. It was probably 70 or 80 miles from Deep Creek. Sam gave me $10 to trail the horses. I made it as far as Munsey Creek and stayed with Orvell Jaceway the first night. The next day I got to the Cleveland ranch with the horses. When I got over there, it was raining and snowing, so I stayed two or three days.

*Jed and Bimbo. Circa 1932.*

One day I decided to head back. It was about one in the afternoon. I started out, and it began to storm. I rode a little bay horse I called Bimbo. I had my slicker and chaps. It was storming, and the mountains were black. I kept coming. It got dark, and I didn't know where I was, but I let the little horse have his head. He'd smell along the ground and keep traveling along. Finally, the horse hit the road above Eight-Mile, and then I knew where I was. The trip home took 11 or 12 hours.

Bimbo was a mustang-cross horse. His mother belonged to John Erickson. John ran the church ranch at that time. A mustang stud had jumped in with his mares, and that's where Bimbo came from. My brother-in-law Sam Littledyke rode that horse out of the Bowery chutes, and the horse bucked so hard that he fell over with Sammy. He kicked free of the horse. Oh, it bruised him up some, but he was all right. The horse was three or four years old. I bought him and broke him to ride.

# Sambo

I wanted a little horse that Sammy owned. As further payment for driving the horses to the Cleveland ranch, Sammy gave me him. When Sammy gave him to me, he wasn't even halter broke. I broke him when he was four or five years old. He was a sorrel horse with a big star and a strip on his face. Sammy had a good mare that they worked and rode, both. A mustang stud came in and got with the mare, and that's where he came from. I called him Sambo.

He was raised in those South Mountains. That horse was the most sure-footed horse I ever rode. He could take me over any rocks and brush. He never stumbled in the mountains and was a peach of a horse. I used to catch a mustang, once in a while, on him. I'd run them off the water back of Parrish's place.

*Gerald and Sambo. Circa 1933.*

Ray Skinner wanted him for his wife Daisy. He'd say, "You gonna sell me that horse today, Jed?"

One day Ray pulled in the yard, just as me and my mother were pulling out of the yard. He offered me $250. I didn't want to sell Sambo very bad, but that sounded like a lot of money to me at the time. I walked down to the corral and put a halter on him. When my mother and I got back, he was gone.

Some doctor in Delta, Utah, had him for a while. Ray used him for a pick-up horse in the rodeos, too. He told me, "Old Sambo can't run very fast, but he can sure cheat like hell and get right in there to pick up the bronco riders."

*Jed and Sambo taking cows to pasture in the McCurdy fields.*
*October 1947.*

# Floyd West

Floyd West was like a father to me, after my own dad died. He and Blanche lived just to the west of the Cook place by a half mile. He always wore a denim coat, with one button at the top done up. He said to watch out for snow from fog—that it's a bad storm if it's foggy first. Sure enough, his prediction was correct, as that started the winter of 1948 and '49.

My mother and I walked to Floyd's place in the winter to listen to the "Amos and Andy" program on the radio. The snow was on the ground. We'd walk home late and run a ways to keep warm.

Floyd liked to come up to the Queen of Sheba where my brother Les had a camp and took care of a herd of sheep. Floyd would fish the creek below. The creek was full of trout in those days. Then he'd bring the fish to camp. Sometimes, he was pretty well lit by the time he got there. He'd fry those fish up and eat them, bones and all. I often wondered if it wasn't the fish bones that contributed to his throat cancer and killed him in the end.

Floyd's girls, Marge and Lorna, were often at my mother's place, ready to go riding with me in the West Hills to look for mustangs. We would watch the horses coming to water and see the stallions roll, paw the dirt, and rear up to fight. Floyd West saw to it that his girls rode good ponies. Margie rode a cute little bay baldy-faced horse, and Lorna rode a brown mustang that I caught as a two-year-old when the horses came to drink in the creek by the old dirt road between our home ranch and West's.

When I caught that horse for Lorna, that was the second time I had my rope on him. The first time was when Lester Weaver and I rode out past the black knoll on a wagon track. We saw a herd of horses feeding in the draw. They didn't see us. I told Lester to sneak around in front of them, so they'd run my way, and I'd try to put a rope on one. I roped this brown colt with two white hind socks. I made a fire, heated up a stick, and tried to brand the colt with a 96. I was drawing the brand on when the colt jerked back and kicked Lester on the leg. I got to laughing so hard that I let the colt get away. Two years later, this same colt came into drink with the gentle horses. He still had a piece of a brand on him. I roped him and gave him to Lorna.

Floyd had an old saddle, and Blanche had a "woman's saddle." Lorna would jump up on her horse and take off running with nothing but a mane hold. One day, Floyd asked her to bring the horses from the meadow to the corral. He needed work horses for something he was doing. The horses took off and ran down by the shearing corrals. Lorna ran as hard as her horse could run to get around them. Her horse fell and rolled over her. We thought it killed her. It scared the hell out of us. She was knocked out for two or three hours. She finally came around.

I got a gray mare from Wade Parrish one time. She had bucked Newell Kelley off, so I got her on a trade. My brother Les had just bought a new saddle, and that was all I had to ride her with. I was afraid of breaking it, so I hooked her up to the buggy. Lorna West was probably 12 years old, and she was standing behind me in the buggy. The mare went to kicking and bucking and peeing. It was just like it was raining. Lorna kept wiping her face with her hands and hollering, "Oh, gawd, oh, gawd!"

When I finally got the mare broke, she was a hell of a good horse. My nephew Doyle was just a kid. He'd come to the ranch and ride with Lorna West and Reid Trimble. I'd tell him not to run that gray mare, 'cause it made her crazy, but I know as soon as they'd get out of sight, they'd race. One day, Reid said, "Boy, that mare sure can run."

I kept her for a good long while. She was gray, but she turned white. One day Bill Ketchum came along. I needed some money so I sold her to Bill for $45.

*L to R: Blanche West, Floyd West, Will Cook, Ruth Pomeroy, and Audrey Cook. Circa 1900.*

Lorna was full of hell. Florence Kelley worked for my mother in the hay field, driving a team and raking hay. Lorna and Reid were just kids. They were sent to the spring to fill a jug with water. Lorna caught a little frog and dropped it in the jug. They handed the jug to Florence and backed off. Florence was big enough she could have killed both of them. I don't recall if she drank the frog or not.

Wes Featherstone used to have a camp and corrals by the water in Round Valley or Little Valley. I would go up and stay with Wes sometimes. Floyd's son Bill West and I used to put a straw in a frog's behind and blow it up. Then we'd turn it loose on the water. They were helpless to go under and would just sort of move their legs around and croak.

# Wes Featherstone

William and Elathine Kelley homesteaded the Kelley place. After Bill blowed his head off with a 12-gauge shotgun, Mrs. Kelley married Featherstone, and they had Wes.

My mother and my dad worked for Mrs. Featherstone when Wes was a baby. My dad couldn't do much because he was crippled. She paid my parents $1.50 a week plus room and board.

Wes was about 14 years older than me. He was the same age as Sam Littledyke. I sure looked up to him. He lived around the valley in his sheep camp. He never married until he was 65 or 70 years old. He lived in Twin Falls, Idaho, and died there too.

I used to go with Wes Featherstone wherever he was going. He had a herd of horses, and he raised mules in the South Mountains. One spring, he wanted to brand them and castrate the stud mules. He'd front-foot them with a rawhide rope. I'd jump on their heads and hold them down until he could get a rope on their hind feet. I'd get down on that mule's head as close to the ground as I could. The mule's hind feet would be kicking clear past his head. It's a wonder I didn't get my head kicked off. Wes would holler, "Stay with him, Jed, stay with him." Some of them would roll over the top of me and get away too.

I pert-near died once. I had the chicken pox. Wes Featherstone had some horses out in the flat that he wanted to gather up. He came by the ranch. I wanted to go with him. My mother asked my dad if he thought it would be all right. He said he guessed so. I went with him. It was cold and rainy. I caught cold on top of the chicken pox. I damn near croaked, but my parents took me to Mrs. Symonds. She was the doctor around these parts, and she cured me.

41

# Symonds

Times were hard. Old Man Symonds and Mrs. Symonds had a big family. His first name was Stephen, and hers was Jessie. She had been married twice before, but both of her former husbands had been killed with horses. She said she married Stephen because he was too damn slow to be riding horses.

They made their living by selling apples and plums from the big orchard west of their house. One morning the blue jays were squawking. To his wife, Old Man Symonds remarked in his slow-talking way, "Ma, just listen to them laughing jack-asses."

When their daughter Afton was a young girl, the guys would come around chasing her. Mrs. Symonds told her husband, "I'm going to make her some pants made out of tin."

Old Man Symonds slowly replied, "Lord, gawd, Mother! If you did, everybody would be packing can openers!"

Old Man Symonds peddled the fruit around the valley with their team and wagon. He'd would drive up in the yard with his horse and buggy. It took him all day to get out of the wagon.

# Mulners

Old Tom Mulner was a good fellow. He wasn't quite right in the head, but he was good to me. He was always making me a horsehair pad or giving me some little thing. Him and Eph lived with their brother John.

John and Amanda Mulner had four kids—Elva, Jack, Beth, and Margaret. Margaret was hell for playing with snakes. One day at school, Kenny Snively and Oren Probert had been teasing her. She walked the mile to her home in the lane for lunch. When she returned to school, she had a snake in her shirt. Those boys started teasing her again, and she took that big blow snake out. She held it by its neck. Its tongue was going in and out. Those boys sure lit out, and they never teased her no more.

Tom and Eph were brothers. They had both been married, but were bachelors when I knew them. One day they had a fight. Ephie had one arm. He put a wagon burr in a sock and hit Tom. Tom said, "The ol' bastard hit me right in the tit."

One time, Tom Mulner rode the train to Gold Hill. When asked by the engineer if it was true that sheepherders have affairs with them sheep, Tom replied, "Why, Christ yes! Where do you suppose we get our conductors?"

Tom Mulner took care of Wes Featherstone's horses. Wes told Tom, "Ride that mare if you want—she's gentle." Tom got on, and the mare bucked him off. I saw him the next day and asked him what happened. His face was all skinned and scraped up. He said, "Well, my face went in the dirt, and my feet went out West."

Tom Mulner and Roy Hicks (Jay's uncle) got in a fight over water. Roy threw Tom in the creek. When Tom climbed out, he told Roy,

"You little bastard, you told me I couldn't have any water, but I got my pockets full!"

I was gone from Deep Creek for a spell. When I returned, I asked Tom where Ephie was. He replied, "Well, I don't know for sure. He died, and I don't know which way he went."

# Happy Jack

He came here from Erda, Utah. His real name was John Jackson, but everybody called him Happy Jack. He was an old bachelor. When asked if he ever had a girlfriend, he said, "Well, yes, sir, I had one once. I thought a lot of her. I caught her under the bridge with another fellow, and I never went back."

Jack did odd jobs for people around the valley. He irrigated some and herded sheep. He had a team and wagon and two saddle horses. He'd drive in the yard and settle down with you whether you asked him to or not. One winter after my dad died, he showed up and asked my mother how her potatoes were. We had a lot of potatoes from our garden in the cellar bin. "Well," he said, "I'll go back down to Mr. Sheridan's and get some flour, and I'll spend the winter with you."

He came back with probably 500 pounds of flour and spent the winter with me and my mother. He smoked leaf tobacco in his pipe. He'd sit in front of the box stove and spit. The stove was black with spit. He had a dog and a cat that traveled around with him. He went on a walk all the time—never would let the team trot. It took him all day to get from our place down to Sheridan's store. One day he went out the gate, leading his saddle horse Old Tobe. I followed him. I'd never seen him get on the horse. I kept following him out over the hill. He never did climb on the horse.

Burt Robison and Bill Sellas had been fighting over water rights. They held a hearing in Ely, and Happy Jack was called to the stand as a witness. Every question they asked him was answered the same: "Well, sir, I don't remember."

The judge finally got tired of hearing the same response so he said to Happy Jack, "Mr. Jackson, do you know when the 4th of July is?"

Happy Jack replied, "Well, sir, I don't rightly recall, but I know we get drunk and have a hell of a good time!"

*Gentile Georgetta and Happy Jack at Eight Mile Ranch. Circa 1915.*

He lived in a one-room cabin at the McCurdy place on the west side of Deep Creek. Roy McKee built that cabin. He moved his cabin down to Floyd West's place when he got up in his 90s. He slept with a six-shooter under his pillow every night. He ate with Floyd and Blanche. Floyd sat up with him at night. Bill West and I would "babysit" him during the day. He liked to tell stories, and we liked to listen to them. One morning, I went home about sunup. About 10 in the morning, Floyd came down to my place and told me Jack had died.

# Jack Bartho

Old Jack Bartho was a Spaniard, who lived around these parts as long as I can remember. He spoke real broken English. Most of the time, he stayed in a cabin at Sheridan's store. Mary Sheridan was a young gal then. Mary always wore dresses like most of the women around here did. I never did see her wear pants. There were some pigeons that had a nest of little ones, up in the eaves of the old building with the tin roof to the west of the main house. She had Jack get a ladder and hold it, so she could see the little birds. From up high, she called down to Jack, "Jack, did you see my pigeons?"

He looked up from down below and replied, "I ah see ah one ah pigeon..."

# Harlo Bates

I always liked Harlo Bates. His ranch bordered my mother's to the east. One time they had a bronc in the round pen. Lenard Bates, Harold Kelley, and others stood around deciding who was going to get on. Harlo walked up, put his milk bucket on the post, rode the bucking horse, and went on back to milking the cow.

Once when I was threshing grain, I got a very bad nose bleed. I had to go to the infirmary on the Wendover Air Base. I was gone for at least four days, and Harlo combined my grain.

One winter, as I was riding down the valley horseback, I met Harlo Bates leaving his ranch, heading west on a horse. I said, "Where you going, Harlo?"

He said he was going to Boone Springs to catch the "pony express bus" to Ely. His daughter Eva had just been born. Boone Springs is about 30 miles west of here, as the crow flies or the cowboy rides, on the Ely Highway 93. The year was 1937.

Harlo's boy Lenard and I were chasing wild horses out west one time. I told Lenard to wait until the mustangs got their bellies full and then run right in the middle of them real quick-like. We did just that. I caught a good-sized black colt with a wide strip down his face. I lost Lenard in the chase, so I tied my colt to a tree and tracked Lenard. I followed his tracks down a hollow and out west by the Indian graves in the black hills. His horse was standing there with the reins hanging down. I was worried that the horse had fallen with him. Pretty soon, I caught up with Lenard. When I found him, he was going up a wash holding onto a big colt by its tail. The colt was pulling him along, and he was hanging on for all that he was worth. He'd have been there yet, if I hadn't handed him a rope. We brought those colts home. The Bates ranch had a pole bridge you had to cross to get to their place. Lenard's colt stuck his leg between two poles and broke his leg. I kept my colt for a few days and got it halter broke. My mother didn't like it when I brought mustangs home. She figured they ate up all the feed. I said to her, "You know what I'm going to do with that colt?"

"No," she said, "What are you going to do?"

"I'm going to give him to the Symonds kids," I said. Miller Symonds had the Symonds' place on the east side of the valley. He had a bunch of kids, so I took the colt to them. They were sure tickled.

Later on, I went to visit Miller. He was riding that little black horse around his sheep. His feet were not very far off the ground. When Miller left this valley and moved to Grantsville, he sold the horse to Jay Hicks. That little black horse turned out to be a pretty good horse. Jay's kids took him to Ely in 4-H and around. They called him Comet.

Mabel was Harlo's wife. Her maiden name was Hall. She was a good woman and a real good cook. Her and Harlo raised a big family and took in orphans and everybody else. Harlo milked his cow, and she sent cans of cream on the mail to make a dime. They had a pantry on the east side of their house where the cream separator stood. I can remember the flies being thick in that room and on top of the milk. She'd scrape them off and finish the separating.

Lenard and his mother lived at the Bates ranch alone in later years. One day, they were discussing the time it takes for a chicken egg to hatch. Lenard said to his mother, "Mother, it takes three weeks for an egg to hatch."

She shook her head replied, "No, Lenard, you're not quite right. It takes 21 days for a chicken egg to hatch."

# Fred Kelley

Fred and Sadie Kelley were good old sticks. They lived on Kelley Spring. Kelley Spring is just south of Symonds' place on the east side of the valley.

Fred Kelley and I loved my mother's bread pudding. One day we ate and ate until it was almost gone. Before I married Joyce, Fred Kelly asked, "Hee hee, can she make bread pudding, Jod?"

Another time, Fred was gone sheepherding. Sadie and her daughter Elma tried to start their Model T. Sadie cranked it. The car was in gear, and it ran over her. She was pinned underneath it. Elma jumped on her horse and ran to the Symonds' place for Miller or one of the other boys to help.

When Fred Kelley was older, he went to Magna to work in the copper pit. He lived with his niece in a little clapboard house. It was cold and in the middle of winter. Fred stayed in the back room of this little old house. One night, his niece went in the back room to check on Fred. She said Uncle Fred was in bed. His feet were sticking out over the end. She said, "Uncle Fred, let me tuck your feet in," to which he replied, "Oh no, I don't want those cold sons-of-bitches in bed with me!"

# Roy Murchison

Roy Murchison come here from Texas. I don't know if it's true or not, but he supposedly killed a fellow in Texas and come here to get away. He married Ike Lee's daughter Nora. He moved from place to place working the hay fields. For a time, he lived in a shack on Skinner Spring on the top of Clifton Flat. He had quite a few horses and sheep that he ran on Dutch Mountain. He moved around building reservoirs to catch flood waters so people could water their cattle and sheep.

I broke a little roan mare for him when I was just a kid. She wouldn't weigh 1,000 pounds. He bought her from Dan Probert and sold her to Lloyd Christiansen.

Roy worked in Sanford for Wes Featherstone. Wes paid him in heifers. Roy drove them home. They were young and wild. They split up. I saw him coming by West's place. I saddled my horse and helped him gather them up. We corralled them at my mother's place. Next morning, he wanted to brand them. He branded with an "M," but he said, "Let's brand them boogers across the nose. They made me mad." So we ran a hot bar across their nose. They looked like they were wearing hackamores.

When the WPA come out during the depression, he and Nora moved to Ely, and he went to work with WPA. Nora kept a little bunch of chickens. He said that he had moved around so much that, when Nora's chickens saw him hitching the harness on the team, they'd run and jump in the back of the wagon.

The last time I saw Roy was by the Plaza Hotel in Ely. He was getting kind of old. He told me, "Jeddy, I've moved around lot in my life. I'm gonna make one more move." He pointed towards the Ely cemetery... Within a week he died.

# Gold Hill and Uncle John

Gold Hill was a regular boom town in the early 1900s. The cabin with the rock chimney still stands in Rodenhouse Wash where my mother cooked for the miners when my brother Les was a baby. She worked for a man named Clyde Wilson in the year 1904. My dad did odd jobs there, even though he was so crippled.

Ollie Young had a cabin southwest of the Yellow Hammer Mine. He bootlegged whiskey there and hauled it down to the town of Gold Hill for the miners. Ollie ran a big herd of horses in those gold hills too.

Jack Rice hauled ore out of Gold Hill with a team of six or eight horses and a wagon. Some of these wagon tracks were pretty steep and windy. Jack sometimes couldn't see his lead horses around a bend, but he trusted them.

Gold Hill had a regular stockyards that held the cattle until they could be shipped out by train that came through. The Deep Creek railway came up from Wendover, by the Last Chance Ranch, and then to Gold Hill. I remember riding the train as a little boy. It ran until the 1930s.

My Uncle John Cook ran the drug store and the pool hall in Gold Hill. It really wasn't much of a drug store, but Uncle John sold groceries and ice cream that used to come in on the train. He really didn't sell much. All the kids in the country came in and sat at his counter to eat free ice cream. He was a happy-go-lucky man. Nothing much bothered John. It is said that the reason he was so happy was that he had his own moonshine still in the cellar of the drugstore.

Uncle John practically raised some of the kids around Gold Hill, including Sonny Tripp. Sonny's mother would go on a drunk for days and leave Sonny. Uncle John would see him coming up the dirt road, barefooted, packing his clothes under his arm. He'd take Sonny in and care for him.

Uncle John's boy Worth was my generation. He was full of hell. Worth and I were sitting in the shade of the drugstore one day. A traveler had come across the desert and stopped his car in front of the building. He was pretty dusty. He said, "What a hell of a country this is! How do people live? What do they do for water?"

Old Man Wilfong was shuffling up the wide dirt main street with his walking cane.

Worth sat there for a minute, and then he said, "See that old man walking down the road with his stick? He's just went and got his water. He takes that stick and beats the piss out of lizards with it." The man got back in his car and drove away.

Along about this time, when Gold Hill was booming, two miners were working a jack hammer down a hole. The poisonous gas in the mine killed the men. Some of the miners helped lay the dead men out on a pool table under a sheet in Uncle John's pool hall and waited for the sheriff to arrive. Alec Noble, Stan Kearney, and other miners took turns watching the bodies. In between watches, Worth climbed up onto the table between the two dead men under the sheet. When the guys came into the room with their coal oil lamp to check the bodies, Worth raised up and scared the hell out of those boys, but sure tickled Uncle John.

Blaine Hicks widened out the steep curve below Gold Hill with Jay's new 1937 Chevy. Him and I were headed to a dance in Callao. He was a-singing and not paying attention to the road. We went bouncing down through the desert in that fancy new car.

# Tippetts

Bill and Gus Sellas emigrated from Greece. Gus married Alice Tippetts after her husband, John, died. They had a store and sold groceries and whiskey. Tippetts had a good sheep and cow ranch about 30 miles west of Deep Creek. After Gus and Alice died, their sister Mrs. Marvis came to help. The store and the living quarters was all one building. You stepped down into their kitchen on the south end of the building. You had to step around a long wood table to get to the living room.

I had a combine and put up Bill's grain one year. Mrs. Marvis served soup for lunch. I never will forget when I looked into that pot of soup and saw a sheep's head. The eye stared right at me. I wasn't too sure I wanted to eat Mrs. Marvis' soup.

A hard winter hit in the 1930s. Bill Sellas' cows drifted over towards Deep Creek and my mother's place. They were weak. Some got down in the mud where the creek goes across the corner of the fence. Bill and Old Jack Bartho came to drive them home. Two cows were down and couldn't get up. Bill told my mother she could have those two cows. My brother Les had a homemade sleigh made from the back seat of a Model T. He fashioned some runners on it. Les brought those two poor old cows to the ranch on that sleigh.

# Working to Make a Dollar

I worked at different odd jobs to make a dollar as a teenager. I pulled logs out of the Durst, Eight-Mile, and Kelley Canyons with a team of horses for Uncle Carl Hibbard as he worked his sawmill. He had a contract with the government to build log cabins for the Goshute Indians. Many of those cabins still stand today. Uncle Carl would lead two good work horses up the mountain. He'd cut a log down, tie it behind one horse, and turn him loose. Those horses would bring the logs to the base of the canyon, and then we would load the logs on a wagon and take them to Uncle Carl's sawmill. Those old horses were smart. If the log they were dragging got stuck on a tree or a rock, the horses would turn around and go back up the hill to unloose the log.

Uncle Carl's boy Milt had a spooky mustang horse tied to a tree at the base of the canyon. The horse jumped and kicked Milt in the chest, knocking him out. Uncle Carl loaded Milt on top of the load of logs and brought him back to the house. Milt never came to for two or three days, but he finally got all right.

I hauled 50-gallon drums of oil weighing 400 pounds apiece up the mountain when Dan Probert staked a claim and started mining tungsten at the Cinnabar Mine. Dan fashioned a cart that would hold one drum of oil. It was all my work horse team could do to take that oil up to Dan's mine in the morning and haul an empty down in the afternoon. I got paid $4 per drum.

When I got up there with the oil, I'd go to work for John Mulner. He was a driller at the mine. My job was to turn the drill. It was a big steel pipe that Mr. Mulner would hit with an eight-pound sledge hammer. Bang! Bang! In between each bang, I'd turn the steel. I was pretty nervous at first, but Mr. Mulner was steady, and I trusted him. He never hit my hands with the hammer. Curley

Snively worked there for a short time but soon quit because he was too nervous about getting hit with the hammer. After the day's work, my team of horses would haul the empty drum back down the valley to be sent away on the train and refilled.

*Jed, Selum, and Brownie cleaning ditches*
*and getting bogged down at the Cook ranch. Circa 1937.*

With the same good horses, Old Selum and Brownie, I worked for Fred Snively in his field putting up hay. I drove a team and used a horse-drawn buck rake to rake hay. I'd stack the hay with a Jackson fork. Old Man Probert came after me and wanted me to work for him in the field. He asked how much Fred paid me. I told him $1.50 a day. He said, "Oh hell, I can't afford that. I'll pay you a dollar a day." So, I got disgusted and harnessed up my team to go home. His boy, Carl, caught up with me and said he'd pay me the $1.50.

*Haying with the team. July 1941.*

Arthur Kelley leased Old Man McCurdy's meadow. My mother, Floyd West, and I worked together to put up the meadow hay amongst the three places. There was no money involved. We just did it. Arthur was handy and built a dump rake that was pulled with a team. His wife Florence drove the team.

I herded sheep, sheared sheep, lambed sheep, rode colts for everybody, punched cows, drug ditch, threshed grain, and always traded horses. I rode a derrick horse, helping stack hay, 'til I was so damn tired I thought I'd fall off. In the wintertime, we'd harvest ice in big blocks from Sheridan's pasture. We'd wrap it in sawdust and straw so we could have ice cream in the summertime. My mother and I kept a flock of turkeys to pay the ranch taxes. They are without a doubt the dumbest animal on the face of the earth. And I never liked to milk a damned milk cow.

I always said my life-long piles condition was from riding bareback when I was a kid. When I was young, I didn't own a saddle. Oft times my piles pained me so that I would get off my horse and lay down under a bush on my way to school.

I found out about Santa when I found Old Man McCurdy's McClellan saddle in the cellar where it was waiting for Christmas Day. The saddle was 40 years old then and was made for Charlie Felt's brother, Tori Felt. It was stamped with a TF on the cantle. That was my first saddle, and I was damned glad to have it. Later on, Dan Probert bought it, and it's probably still at the Probert place.

# The Hamley Saddle

A fellow by the last name of Robison used to live in Snake Valley. He was an agent for Hamley saddles. Hamley sold saddles out of Pendleton, Oregon. If you bought a saddle through him, you saved a little money. Melbourne Robison was just a young fellow. He managed the Cleveland Ranch at the north end of Spring Valley. He had ordered a Hamley, and before it came, he went to work down at Swallows in the Minerva Mine. My brother Les worked there for a little while too. When the saddle came in, Melbourne sold it to Les. He let Les have it for just what it had cost him. That was $75. I believe the year was 1937. The cantle of the saddle is stamped with M.A.R. for Melbourne A. Robison. I still have that saddle. It's a damn good bronc saddle, but it has been known to leak at times...

*The Hamley saddle has stood the test of time and is still used on colts today. The Kelly Place in background. 2017.*

# Surveying the Wendover
# Air Force Base

In the fall of 1940, Kenny Snively, Keith Chastain, and I heard about a job in Wendover. We went down and applied to develop the base. There was nothing but a swamp there. We got hired on to drain the slew. I borrowed my brother Les' sheep camp. That's where we lived for the next three years. We were handed gum boots and a shovel. I remember voting on the day we hired on. Hoover was going out of office. FDR was who I voted for, and I claim to be a Democrat ever since. The second or third day of work, my crew told me to go work with a group of other guys who were surveyors, so I went to work surveying. When I filled out my application, I stated that I had helped the survey crew when they surveyed the upper Goshute reservation land. I still remember the length of the runways—14,000 and a little bit more feet.

*Wendover Air Base. Back row: Gerald Cook, 6th from the left;*
*Keith Chastain, 11th from the left; Kenny Snively, 16th from the left. 1940.*

The sheep camp became a regular stopping/sleeping place with boys sprawled sideways on the bed and sleeping on the projections. Curley Nicholes would, on occasion, bring in beef steak or lamb chops. Frank Sorenson's dad Harold told me that he was in heaven eating lamb chops from a sheep camp, as he had been a long-time sheep herder.

One night we come into the sheep camp after working. Kenny was reading his mail in the back of the sheep camp. I loaded the stove with wood so I could cook some supper. Kenny wasn't saying much. Garth Weaver had given us a can of high test gas to get the oil and grease out of our shirts. It was setting to the side of the sheep camp. I poured a little of that gas on the wood, stepped back out of the camp, and threw the match in on top. Whoof! The blast blew all the wood out of the stove. When the black smoke cleared, I could see little fire flames floating in the air and close to the camp ceiling. Kenny come out of the back hollering, "What the hell you trying to do?" I got him up off the bed anyway.

We were paid $4 a day and thought we were rich. When we got our first paychecks, we went to Mantes Chevrolet in Tooele and bought new Chevys. Kenny's was a Chevy coupe, and mine was a sedan. We paid $1,100 each.

While we were in Tooele, we signed up for the army. They temporarily deferred me on account of my mother being a widow and having a ranch. It went on for a while. I kinda wanted to go. I sold my new car, thinking I was going. I went into the office again. Old Man Amos Bevan was on the board. They decided to defer me from the army permanently at that time.

# My Brother Dies at age 36

While working in Wendover in 1941, the call came in that my brother Les had passed away. Alec Nobles would not let me come back to Ibapah by myself. I have much respect for Alec Nobles. Les had had a cold. He went down to the barn to harness the team and feed the cows. A severe pain hit him in the back. He lay around for a couple of days, and Mother doctored him with mustard plasters. She got so worried about him that she had Wade Calloway come and take him to Ely. He was in the Ely hospital for a week or 10 days. The doctors told my mother that Les had pneumonia, but that she had nearly cured it with her home remedies. He was scheduled to be released that day. Mother was in the lobby going out of the hospital. when the nurse came running to tell her that he had just died. The doctor later concluded that a piece of pneumonia had broken loose in his lung and hit his heart.

*Les sporting Goshute-made buckskin gloves.*

# Sammy, Mary, and I Help Out

I quit my surveying job and came home to help my mother on the ranch. She always worried about the way things were being done. I grew a field of grain. Harlo Bates told me to hold the water off until the bottom leaves turned yellow and then to turn the water to it. If you water it all the time, you just get a lot of straw. Audrey had to confer with Harlo to make sure I was doing it correctly. He told her, "Leave him alone, Audrey, the boy knows what he is doing." It was the prettiest stand of grain, not very tall, but with a good head on it that threshed up well.

*Jed and Audrey. July 1942.*

Sam and my sister Mary Littledyke homesteaded in the South Mountains in Sanford Canyon. Sammy was good to come down in the summers and help with the hay. They had their boys, LeRoy and Doyle, at that time. Sammy was a hard-working man. He built a two-room cabin, two nice round corrals, a good reservoir, and a mile of fence to separate his section from Georgetta's ranch. There was only a steep wagon trail that went up over Sanford and into Pleasant Valley. Cars could not travel it. Sam and I hooked a walking plow to a team of horses and built a road around the mountain, down into Rye Grass, and into Pleasant Valley. I stood on the doubletrees and drove the team. The plow wouldn't really plow because it was so rocky. It would dig up rocks so we could move them by hand out of the way. I was standing on the doubletrees, and I would go flying up between the horses when the plow loosened the rock.

*Jed. July 2, 1942.*

On one occasion, Sherm and Beth Cook were visiting Sam and Mary. Les had a Model T Ford. He drove it by the reservoir, and the car slid sideways off the road. Les was sitting in it talking to

Sherm, when the ground gave away, and the Model T tipped over, trapping him underneath. Sherm and Sam righted the car off Les, beings as Model Ts aren't very heavy. The battery was on top of him. The acid ate his coat, and he suffered from stinging nettle bites. It scared him pretty good.

They eventually sold out to Wade Parrish for $1,000. Wade ended up with seven sections of 640 acres purchased for $1,000 each. He ran 1,500 head of sheep on those seven pieces of ground. After some years, he sold his herd of sheep and seven grazing homesteads of ground to Fawn Henroid from Pleasant Valley for $40,000.

My sister Mary and her husband Sammy went to work for the Cleveland Ranch in Spring Valley. She had a baby there. Mary and Maime Clover were doing the washing. The baby was asleep in his crib. When it was time to feed him, Mary went to wake him and found him dead. That Indian lady took off on the run, ran a mile or two to the fields where her husband Frank Eagle and Sam were working the hay, and told them the sad news.

# Memorable Trips to Wendover

Around 1947, Bill Ketchum bought a bunch of horses from people around the valley. Jay Hicks and I drove the horses to Wendover to put them on the train. We started out about 7 o'clock a.m. and were in Wendover by 2 o'clock p.m. We were held up by the guards at the gate, as we had to pass through the base to get to the stockyards. Jay tried to reason with the guards, while I tried to hold the horses. I had a hell of a time holding them. I had a good work horse that had eaten loco weed and become locoed. Pat was his name. He was in the herd. A guy drove past and honked his horn. Old Pat jumped and kicked the radiator out of his car.

*Jed Cook and his first truck, a 1947 Chevy purchased from Dick Heinbaugh at the Chevrolet garage in Ely, Nevada. Sold to Devaney garage in Wendover, Utah. Picture is taken on Hogs Back. October 1947.*

Finally, we got them to the stockyards. We spent the night in Wendover and saw to it that the horses were loaded onto the train the following morning.

I went to Wendover in my truck one time. I bumped into Cy Hughes. He ran a service station in Wendover. He wanted my truck so I sold it to him for $700. After I did that, I thought, "How in the hell am I going to get back to Deep Creek now?"

I remembered that Soph Littledyke was staying in Wendover with the kids in school. I was lucky enough to catch up with Al. He had come in to visit her and get a load of coal. We went up to the Nevada Club and drank up most of my truck money. When it was gone, we headed home along towards sunup. It was winter and cold. We stopped on Rocky Ridge, and Al got out of his truck, saying, "I forgot about my pigs!"

He had been given some little half-starved pigs. Al had put those little pigs in a gunny sack and tossed them up on top of the load of coal earlier that night. He reached up and grabbed the sack. The poor little pigs were froze solid from the cold night ride.

# Rodeos

Dan Lee and I chummed around a lot and thought we were bronc riders. He was girl crazy. He fell in love with a school teacher in Pleasant Valley. Helen Collis was her name. She was from McGill. We were probably 15 at the time. He wanted me to go with him to see Helen. She was pert-near old enough to be his mother.

One time, Dan and I were in Sanford herding sheep. Some stray horses came into water. There was a team and a couple of others. One horse had saddle marks on him, but was real snorty. We snubbed him up to my horse, and Dan got on. He said, "If he bucks me off, you gotta give him a try." I said I would. There were two reservoirs—one was dry, and one was full of water. We held him in that dry reservoir where it was good and level. I handed Dan the halter rope. About the second jump, Dan went up as high as he could go. He was wearing some batwing chaps. I can see those batwing chaps flying yet.

One hand scooped up a handful of dirt, and I'll be damned if that horse didn't come up under him. Every jump Dan was bucked off. He was behind the saddle and then up on his neck and every which way. Somehow that horse would come up underneath Dan every time. He bucked into the reservoir filled with water, and Dan kind of got him stopped. Then down the canyon he went. I raced and caught up with him. The horse had only a halter on his head, and Dan was trying to hold him with the halter rope. I've never seen a bronc ride like that before or since.

Later on, I told Ray Skinner about the horse. He said he knew that horse. He was a bucking horse from town that nobody in there could ride. The marks were from a packsaddle. Once you had a bridle on this horse, he had a pretty good rein on him and was a traveling fool.

Stewart Sheldon and I were working in Wendover for a time. We decided to go to a rodeo on our day off. It was hot and in the summertime. We were traveling across the Salt Flats to a rodeo by the railroad tracks in Ogden. Stewart bought a bottle of gin. We drank warm gin across the flats with no chaser. We got to where the rodeo was being held, and Stewart high-centered on a rock. We walked down the hill to the rodeo. The announcer was asking, "Will anybody ride this bull?" Stewart hollered that he would... in fact, he and I would ride it double! Stewart rode it frontwards, and I rode it backwards. I was bucked off at the get-go, but stout old Stewart would reach down and pull me back on every time I was falling off.

I've often talked about how much fun Ned Christiansen was when he was a boy. Once there was a rodeo up the canyon in Tooele. A guy who was a teacher then was announcing. His name was Max Gowans. Ned was the clown. When I arrived, the two of us went down to the creek where Ned had a jug of whiskey hid out. The rodeo was one of those little amateur affairs. Ed Gillispie, the stock contractor, told me there were only two tough ones to ride in the whole herd. Max Gowans called out my name, and sure enough he called out the big gray gelding, one of the tough ones. Max announced, "Look at that kid from Deep Creek ride!"

I lost my attention and fell off. Ned and I went back to the creek, and just as we were coming back up the hill, Max called me again—and darned if I didn't get the rank bay mare. I rode her. They were going to put me on a big bay work horse mare, but Ed Gillispie stepped up and told the guys that were running it that they were cowards for giving a guy that had just driven 200 miles the rankest horses they had.

# Winter of 1948 - '49

It was early February 1949, a winter that folks still talk about. Jay Hicks and I had some cows out west that we had to check on. He had a horse trailer and a Jeep, so we were going to load our horses in the trailer and drive out to check on our cows. I left for Hicks' ranch on horseback about 1 o'clock in the afternoon. It was 10 o'clock when I hit the hill above Hicks where I met Darryl Wadsworth and Kenny Antry in an army snowplow. There was just enough room to squeeze between the plow and a 20-foot-high snow bank to get through. I spent the night at Hicks' place, and in the morning, Jay and I tried to start an old Jeep, but it wouldn't turn over. Hell, we built a fire under it, and it still wouldn't go. We went to the house to warm up. Jay had a thermometer on the wall of the house. It read 40 below. Since we couldn't get the Jeep to go, we set out on horseback looking for cows. You couldn't tell where solid ground was. Your horse might walk out onto a drift, and would flounder around until it got out. Jay was riding a spooky little sorrel horse. He was dressed in army issue clothes that his brother Blaine had given him—a cap with big long ear flaps on his head, big wide army brogues, and he was wearing electrical army surplus pants! We were walking behind a little bunch of cows, leading our horses. Jay went to put his foot in the stirrup, and the horse spooked and spun around with Jay sticking out like a blade on a propeller. When he came loose, he landed in a big snow bank. I laughed and told him, "Any man that would ride a horse in that get-up ought to fall off his horse."

"Creeest, I guess you're right." Jay said.

# Pinto

I got Pinto from a guy that took care of Burt Robison's sheep. Burt had a big herd of sheep that he ran north of Tippetts, out in the flats. I can't remember this guy's name, but we were always trading something. One day I rode through his camp. He said, "Jed, I'm leaving Burt and going to Oregon to buy a dairy. I'm selling my horses. There's only two guys in these parts that I'd sell my horses to. That's Melbourne Robison and Jed Cook."

He had a pretty good-looking roan horse and a pinto. I hurried home to get my trailer. I wasn't thinking too much about the pinto, but more about the roan. Melbourne beat me to him. I bought this sorrel pinto horse for $75. I brought him home. He had been trailered around and was kinda tired. I saddled him up, and damn, he was a nice horse. He had a good rein on him, light in the mouth. I let him rest up a few days and climbed on. He went to bucking. He'd buck and sunfish, turning his old belly up. He'd come close to falling, but he never did. He'd throw his head back and hit the stirrup one jump. The next jump, he'd throw his head and hit the stirrup on the other side. He bucked me off several times. I rode him for five or six years. When he bucked, he meant business. He meant to get you off too. He was so damned crooked.

Lester Weaver was helping me with the derrick horses and the Jackson fork stacking hay one summer day. Floyd's girls Lorna and Marge were at the place too. Three soldier boys from the Wendover base drove into the yard in an army Jeep and stopped when they saw the girls. One boy hopped right up on the hay. He knew how to handle a Jackson fork. It was hot, and he took off his shirt. Old Pinto was standing down by the corral. The soldier asked if he could ride him. I told him that Pinto could buck a little and wasn't too gentle. Lorna and Marge kept pestering me to let him ride him. They caught the horse and helped get him saddled up. That boy climbed aboard. Old Pinto took a couple of jumps, and he fell off. "I wasn't ready," he said. So he got back on, and Old Pinto went to bucking, and he meant business now. That soldier landed on his bare back in the gravel there in the yard. He didn't have no hide left on his back. We took the guy down under the trees by the pond. He was hurt pretty bad. His soldier buddies loaded him in the Jeep and took him back to Wendover. I heard he was laid up for a good long while.

When the government bought the Georgetta place on the Eight-Mile side for the Goshute Indians, it was the 4th of July, and they held a big celebration. I rode Old Pinto over there a-horseback. Lyle Sabey from Callao was sitting there in a car. He had had a few drinks, and he wanted to get on behind my saddle. I told him no, and then I had a few drinks with him. When we ran out of whiskey, we went to Tippetts to get some more.

By then, I had just enough whiskey that I decided to let him on. We were out in the corral to the southwest of the house where the derrick stood. He climbed on, and Pinto went to bucking. Lyle's big fist came around and hit me square in the mouth. He fell off. I looked down at Lyle. He was kind of a big man. He looked 20 feet long laying there. I tried to pull my horse up, but I couldn't. He bucked until I fell off too. We sure put on a show for all those folks at the 4th of July party.

They held a dance that night. Frank Lee and others were laughing about Lyle and me getting bucked off Old Pinto. Frank said he'd bet $100 that anybody in this valley except Jed Cook couldn't ride that pinto horse. I said, "Sometimes Jed Cook can't ride him either."

*Jed and Ol' Pinto. Circa 1940.*

One morning, Dee Heckathorn and another fellow from Spring Valley showed up at the ranch. This fellow was contracting calves. My mother made lunch, and afterwards we stepped outside. Pinto was tied to the corral. This fellow said, "You know I had that horse overnight, and he damn near killed me. I bought that horse from Irwin Hesslegesser. I got to thinking that I never did see Irwin or the boys riding him. They were always leading him."

Ray Skinner was in the rodeo business. He traded me two good unbroke colts for Pinto. It was that hard winter of 1948 and '49. Ray's herd of horses and Pinto went out in the West Hills. I went up and put some hay out on the feed ground. The next morning, I found Pinto laying dead where I had fed. I guess he got the belly ache and died. I'd sure liked to see somebody ride him out of a chute.

# The Thomas Place

The Thomas Place is named after Old John Thomas. After he died, his brother came from Missouri and sold it to Bill Chastain. His wife was the postmaster at the time, and she had embezzled some government funds in her post office. Bill sold it to Vic Lawrence of Grantsville to bail her out for $4,000. My mother and I bought the place from Vic before I was married.

*L to R: Bert Baldwin, Blaine Baldwin, John Thomas, and his dog, Goldie. Circa 1929.*

The fence and windmill were down and in bad need of repair. Wade Parrish and I decided we would fix it up. George Knight and Wynn Murphy helped put up the posts, and Wade bought the wire. I went to Salt Lake and bought a windmill. It was in a box and needed to be assembled. Carl Hibbard put it together and put it up for me. Frank Lee and I hauled rocks and manure to dam the creek so I could get the water out on the fields. After Joyce and I were married, we built a road around the west side to get into the Thomas place. It was a good setup. We had plenty of pasture between that place and my mother's place. A few years after Joyce and I were married, her mother persuaded her to sell the Thomas place to the Parrish estate. Joyce finally gave in, and we sold it to them for $7,000.

Earl Hibbard told this story about me:

> *It wasn't long after Audrey and Gerald had bought the Thomas place. Jed was down cleaning ditch with the tractor when he got stuck. A herd of cows were curious, hanging around. Jed waited until the bull walked close enough by, threw a rope on him, tied hard and fast to the tractor, set the dogs on the bull, and pulled himself out of the mud.*

# Courting Joyce

Joyce was a lot younger than me. I helped her dad out a lot. I'd ride derrick horse or help him with sheep or hay. She was always following me around. She was horse crazy and liked to get down around the corrals.

I chased around with her sister Phyllis some, but Joyce was the girl for me.

*Joyce Parrish. Circa 1945.*

She went away to school. First, she went to high school in Lehi. Then she went to Westminster College, BYU, and Utah State. On several occasions, after she had been home to the ranch, I drove her back to school. She was dating a guy from Grantsville named Cliff Lawrence. She was staying at Wade and Chloe's apartment in Salt Lake. Cliff was chasing her. I was staying downtown at the Moxum Hotel. She came and stayed with me to get away from Cliff.

When Joyce and I were dating, we once were riding through Round Valley. I was riding on a little black mustang mare. I ran up over the hill, got off my horse, lay down, and dusted myself up so she thought I was hurt. She was pretty upset, and then she was mad for a little while.

When she went to school in Logan, I stayed with my cousin Jess and his wife Agnes Cook. Joyce told me she was tired of school. I brought her back to Deep Creek. She done the proposing. She was tired of that education business and just wanted to live in the country. One time I was in town and bought a load of coal. I bought her a ring too. It was wintertime, and we got caught in the damnedest blizzard. We got as far as Grantsville and stayed with Sherm and Beth Cook. They leased a service station west of Grantsville from Jess Charles. Sherm told me, "You're not going home in this." Beth had a niece staying with them. Her name was Joyce, too. Joyce slept with her. I stayed in the same bed with an old trapper, who was well known around Grantsville. I can't remember his name.

When we got to Parrish's, Joyce walked in and showed her dad the ring. "Gad, that's beautiful!" Wade said to her.

He slapped me on the knee and said, "That's a beautiful ring. Just be good to her."

*Joyce Parrish on Tony. Circa 1945.*

Before we were married, Joyce taught school in Wendover. She drove out to see me and brought her neighbor and his wife. I had a pup on my porch. This fellow commented on that pup being a good-looking pup. I told him I got the pup from my cousin Jess Cook in Avon, Utah. The guy's eyes grew big. He said, "You know Jess Cook?"

I said, "Well, he's a cousin of mine."

"He's a cousin of mine too!" this fellow said.

That's how I found out I had another cousin in Don Hunter. He was a cowboy, now. He and Wanda had a home in Soda Springs, Idaho, but he was working for some sheep outfit this particular winter. Sheep men used to move the sheep back and forth. They weren't supposed to graze on one spot too long, so Don hired on to herd sheep around Wendover for the winter. They went home not long after. He had a ranch and a herd of cows there. In the winters, they went to Arizona, and he worked for a dude ranch.

They traveled back and forth between Arizona and Soda Springs. He complained to Wanda one day that she had too much stuff to pack, and it took too long to get going. He said, "Before I got Wanda, all I had to do was piss on the fire, call the dog, and be gone."

*Joyce Parrish and Jed Cook. 1949.*

Joyce and I took a trip to Soda Springs, Idaho, to visit Don and Wanda Hunter. We met a man there, I can't remember his name, but he owned a large herd of sheep. He said Wade Parrish came west in the winter and herded sheep for him. He went back east to his home in North Carolina in the summer. He did that for several seasons. One season while sheepherding he went to a dance in Deep Creek and met Chloe Felt there. He herded sheep for George Felt then and ended up marrying his daughter.

Don Hunter was 40 years old when he had a heart attack while in Arizona. They went home to Soda Springs. He wouldn't stay down and take it easy like the doctor told him. He had a stroke and died soon after. Jess Cook and I were pallbearers at his funeral.

*Don and Wanda Hunter and his Dodger with his trophies. Circa 1950.*

*Early sheepherders near Soda Springs, Idaho.*
*Wade Parrish on the mule. Circa 1903.*

*Wedding photo. 1st Presbyterian Church, Elko, Nevada. June 17, 1950.*

Joyce and I got married in the Presbyterian Church in Elko, Nevada, on June 17, 1950. A preacher by the name of Shriver, who traveled around the country, drove up from Carson City to marry us. Joyce's folks, my mother, Joyce's sister Phyllis and her husband

Rao, my sister Mary and her husband Sam, and Charlie Felt were there. Mary and Sam stood up with us for the ceremony. Afterward, Wade bought everybody dinner in one of those places in Elko. The waitress brought wine and put it on the table, if you wanted it. Neither Mary, Sam, Phyllis, nor Rao would drink any of it, but Mr. Shriver raised his glass of wine with us. He wouldn't take any pay for the ceremony, even after driving that far.

Al and Soph Littledyke and Hugh and Chloe Rosenlund came to Elko to separate us and play tricks on us, but we got out of there quick. We went to Reno and then up through Oregon and Washington. Then we came back home through Idaho. We were gone for a week or 10 days.

When we got home, we had a big wedding dance. Uncle Bob Cook, Pat Cook, Frank Butler, Zeke Hammond, and a couple of other fellows came from Grantsville and played for the dance. It went on all night. The next morning, when we went up home, those Grantsville fellows were laying all over on the grass and every-where. They come around, and boy, did the music start up then!

*Chloe Parrish & Wade Parrish fishing in Birch Creek. July 1940.*

After we were married, we'd go fishing on the Callao side of the mountain, up Birch Creek with her folks. Wade was quite the fisherman. We were setting up camp, and Wade dipped the coffee pot in the ditch. I'll be damned if he didn't catch a fish in the coffee pot. That creek was full of trout.

# Peek-A-Boo and Spook

When we were first married, we lived in a little wood cabin on the Cook ranch. Don Hunter had sold me a tall, bay American Saddlebred-cross gelding. I called him Peek-A-Boo. Damn, he had a gait. You could handle him with a twine string.

He'd get so excited waiting to chase the mustangs off the waterhole that he'd stick his front leg straight out in front of him. My horse and dog both used to love to chase the mustangs. I'd hide in the cedar trees and wait for the horses to tank up on water so they'd be easier to catch. I'd have to take the bit out of Peek-A-Boo's mouth because he'd grab it and chew it. He was so damn noisy, I thought they'd spook and run. I'd have a hell of a time holding both my dog and my horse while waiting. I caught a lot of mustangs with him. I'd catch them on the waterhole back of Parrish's ranch. If the horse didn't look too bad, I'd take it home. My mother would raise hell. She didn't want the damn mustang eating up all the feed.

*Joyce with Tobe in our honeymoon cabin at the Cook ranch. Circa 1951.*

*Jed, Peek-A-Boo, and Tobe. Circa 1950.*

I got another horse from Ray Skinner. He came from Lund, Nevada. He was out of a gentle mare and some hot-blood stallion. He was a little brown gelding, probably didn't weigh 1,000 pounds. He was three or four years old when I got him. I broke him and called him Spook. He was a good-gaited little bugger. When he got gentle, I gave him to Joyce so we could have these two nice geldings as a matched set.

The match was short lived. We had been to town and came home to find Spook laying dead in the pasture. A picket fence separated our field from Floyd West's. Spook had either been playing or fighting with horses across the fence. He reared up and ran one of those picket fence posts through his breast.

*Gerald and Spook. Circa 1951.*

Not long after that, I rode Peek-A-Boo through the field east of the house to fix fence. Bate's cows had run through the wire, and it was scattered all around. I got off my horse and started gathering up the wire in front of me. A piece of wire touched Peek-A-Boo, and he started kicking and jumping, getting tangled up in that damned barbed wire. It scared me. I didn't want to get tangled up in it too. I let him go, and he ran down in the south end of the pasture, kicking with the wire strung out behind. When I got to him, he was standing under a tree with his head down, the blood gushing down his leg. He had damn near cut off his right front leg up next to his shoulder. I felt so bad. I just pulled the saddle off him and walked to the house. He was dead in less than 20 minutes.

# Wade Parrish and the Roulette Table

I think the year was 1951 when Wade Parrish drove in the yard. He asked me if I wanted to go to the Taylor Grazing meeting in Ely with him. I decided to go. The meeting was in a shack at the back of a Basque bar called Greg's Club. Art Yelland from Spring Valley and Bill Sellas from Tippetts attended the meeting. It never lasted very long. When we went out, we went through Greg's Club. We stopped and had a few drinks. After that we went to the Bank Club. Wade started playing roulette. Back then, they paid you in real silver dollars. He soon had a big stack of silver dollars in front of him. We decided to go eat. It was getting along towards morning. Art, Bill, and I went into eat, but Wade never did come. When he finally came in, he was broke. He borrowed money from Bill. I remember Bill Sellas pulled a roll of bills out of his bib overalls and peeled off $500 for Wade. He went back to the tables, and I'll be damned if he wasn't back in 30 minutes with Bill's money, and he had made his back as well. We got a room at the Nevada Club. I had to help Wade with his shoes and clothes. He flopped back on the bed and said, "Gad, if Chloe could see me now."

*Wade Parrish and Jed Cook. July 3, 1942.*

87

# Cowboying for Short Pay

After Joyce and I were married, we helped run the Cook family ranch. Joycelyn was born in 1954. Joyce was in the hospital, and Betty Ruth Lange came from Wendover to tell me. I got in there about noon, and Joycelyn wasn't born until the next day. It was a hard birth. Joyce's mother, Chloe, was concerned that Joycelyn would not be normal, with my sister Mary's boy, Leroy, being the way he was. Mary had a hard birth with him, and so he had a slow mind.

Conchi was a Basque girl that was raised in Ibapah. Conchi and Burt lived in one of the apartments in town. I told Conchi about Chloe's concerns. Conchi had been to the hospital already. She said, "Gerald, don't you worry. There's nothing wrong with that baby, and Joyce is all right too!"

It seemed I couldn't quite do things to suit my mother on the ranch. She leased the place to Ray Skinner, so I went to work cowboying for the 3C Ranch south of Ely. Joyce and I moved to the 3C ranch with Joycelyn.

Lee Whitlock and I worked together a lot. We were gathering up some steers in Duck Creek, trailing them back down to the ranch. We had our lunch on our saddles. It was getting late in the day, and we hadn't eaten yet. Lee's horse heard the paper rattling, as he unwrapped his sandwich. The horse was getting tired too, and he kept nickering. Lee always fed him bread and stuff, so the horse reached his head around, and Lee fed him his sandwich.

The 3C ranch sold all their cows and leased the ranch to a California outfit that ran 1,800 head of steers. They kept me on, and one of my jobs was to break their colts. They had some fancy-blooded colts that weren't even halter broke. There was another guy that was supposed to help me.

It was New Year's Day. Joyce and I took off to Burley, California, to get him. We got to a big place that had a hotel and café all in one. We rented a room and went to bed. Early the next morning, I told Joyce, "I'm going down to the café to see if I can find this guy."

A smaller cowboy in an old Levi coat walked up to me. He said, "Say, I'm looking for a fellow I'm supposed to go to work for. You wouldn't happen to be him..."

I said, "Well, I guess I am."

He was probably 70 years old with a Texas drawl. His name was John Hamilton. He had a wife and two kids. We loaded them up, horse and all, and headed for Nevada. That horse never had a hair on him, being raised in that California country. We got to the ranch in the middle of the January night. The horse was shivering and shaking when we unloaded him from the trailer. I told John he better put that horse in the barn. I said, "He'll freeze to death."

"Oh, that spooky son-of-a-bitch, you couldn't put him in the barn!" John proclaimed. That horse shivered around for 10 days or so until his hair started to grow in.

We had that big bunch of steers on open range and in the pastures split around. John and I would ride out in the field to see them. They'd buck around. They were getting fat. Old John would move his horse off kind of easy and start to whistle a little tune. I'll be damned if those steers wouldn't start to follow him right along into the next pasture. I'd trail along behind, and they'd follow John.

John would sometimes tie his stirrups together underneath the horse's belly so, if a horse bucked, he wouldn't lose his stirrups. He liked to drink a little. One day, he saddled up that yellow horse and went out around the steers to get away from his wife while he was on the bottle. The horse came back to the ranch without him.

The road crew were working on the road on Conner's Pass. They found John lying in the bar pit and put him in their truck and brought him back to the Three C Ranch. We hauled him into the Ely hospital 'cause he was hurt so bad. He was pretty broken up, ribs and shoulder busted. He claimed the horse fell down with him.

When John was mended enough to get around some, he came down to the house where I was staying. He said, "You want to buy that horse. I've got to tell you—he bucked me off. He didn't fall down with me."

# Blondie

I said, "No I don't want that horse." One early morning I caught him and saddled him up. I got on him kinda careful like. His old ears went up. I felt him tighten up. I just sat there on him kinda quiet. We moved off slow, and when he got warmed up, he was all right. He could really travel and had a good rein on him. John wanted $250 for the horse, but I didn't have it. I went to Al Littledyke in Ely and borrowed the money. Ol' Blondie was a good horse, but if you got off to open a gate, he'd look around at the coat on the back of the saddle, and he'd go to bucking. He'd buck, but he didn't buck that hard. Even if you rode him every day, you'd saddle him up in the mornings, and he'd be a little humpy. He was a dark-dappled palomino with an iron-grey mane and tail. He was a damn good cow horse.

Marilyn was born when I worked at the 3C ranch. Joyce was in Salt Lake expecting her. I got word that she had arrived, but we had two feet of snow at the 3C ranch. It was October 29, 1957. We were trying to ship steers, and the trucks were stuck all around. When I did finally make it into Salt Lake, Joycelyn wanted to come home with me. She was three years old.

We were still snowed in back at the ranch with a big bunch of steers to feed. There was a Cat plow, but neither Lee Whitlock nor I knew how to start it, but we knew how to hitch the team and wagon, so we fed the steers with the work horses. Pretty soon, a hand named Red showed up and started the Cat. We had to take Joycelyn with us to feed, and she wanted to go. My mother came and stayed on the ranch to help take care of Joycelyn until Joyce and the baby came home.

Moneyed guys from California owned the joint. One day, we were loading some steers. I got paid extra for riding these guys' colts.

But on that day, I needed Ol' Blondie to work the corrals and cut out steers. The boss told John Hamilton he didn't want me riding my horse. I should only be riding their colts. I told John that, if my horse had to go, then I was going too. I quit the 3C ranch right there and then.

# Short Stay at Kennecott Copper

In the fall of 1958, we moved to Ely, Nevada. We lived in a little place back of Junction Motors. Uncle Carl's boy Eldred was a boss at Kennecott. He helped me get a job as a switchman on the train from Ruth to McGill. That was the laziest goddamn bunch of fellows I ever seen. They'd come to work, roll up their coats under their heads, and go to sleep. I didn't stay long. Dave was born in Ely on January 20, 1959.

Stewart Sheldon came to Ely with his mother Cora and his wife Marge. We went on a pretty good party. We got pretty drunk. We went up to the hospital. The nurses weren't going to let us in, but we went right on in and saw baby Dave anyway. Stewart, Marge, and Cora went back to Deep Creek about 4 o'clock in the morning. I had to go to work that morning, and boy, was I sick. I was nervous and jumpy. I remember walking along the railroad tracks to switch the trains. Some of those fellows that worked with me kicked up some dirt. I jumped and spooked like a mustang horse.

# Cowboying in Montana

Pete Johansen was a rancher from down around Milford, Utah. He sold his ranch and his sheep and bought a place near Wisdom, Montana. He offered me a job. I went to see what it looked like, and it looked pretty good to me. Joyce was excited to get out of Ely, and so was I, so we went. Pete said, "I just want you to cowboy, no haying—just taking care of about 900 head of cattle." We bought hay in Dillon. Pete rented us a nice apartment in Dillon to spend the winter. He hired Sherm Cook's boy Glen to come and help be the chore boy.

When we unloaded cows off the trucks, it was a mess. They had loaded cows and calves together. We lost a lot of calves, being trampled to death on the trip from Utah to Montana. Those cows damn near froze to death. On June 1st, there were snow banks all around. There was feed coming on the hills. I finally got them settled down pretty good. Pete came up and wanted to brand. The calves were just getting on their feet, so I didn't want to, but we did. After we branded, Joyce made dinner. Then Pete went out to get his horse and told me to get mine. I asked him what he was going to do. He said he wanted to trail the cows to the higher range three or four miles away. The snow was still deep. I told him, "If you're gonna do it, you're gonna do it by yourself."

I can remember Pete's pipe quivering up and down. He finally said, "Well, I guess you're right." There was an old Montana cowboy there that told Pete I was right. He said you couldn't put them in that high pasture that early in the year.

Pete's place was a few miles out of Wisdom, Montana. That's where I took care of his cows during the summertime. There was a fellow name of Frank Pendleton, who lived just up the road from us. He ran about 1,000 head of cows. One day, he rode into his place on his sorrel, stocking-legged horse he called Boots. He pulled the bridle off, but left the saddle on. The horse wandered over in the yard. There was a well, covered with timber, and the horse fell in–hind-quarters first. Frank come to get me to help get the horse out. We put a loader over the hole and tried to pull the horse out, but the saddle kept getting hung up on the bricks in the well. So I climbed down in the well far enough to undo the saddle from the horse. We put a rope around his middle and up through his front legs. We was finally able to pull him out. Old Frank looked down the well. Horse turds was floating on the water. He said, "Well, Boots, I'm glad to get you out of that well, but you didn't have to shit in it, did ya?"

After Don Hunter died, Wanda remarried. She came to visit us on the ranch for the 4th of July. She was a nice lady with a cute little girl. Her new man commented that there wasn't much excitement on the place, no fireworks or anything. Glen Cook had gathered up some old sticks of dynamite that had been laying around in the fields. Ranchers used to blow up beaver dams some time back. He had a burlap sack full of Giant powder in one of the old back cabins. Glen went and got it. He put the sack of powder down in the field a hundred yards or so. We shot at it with a .22 rifle. It wouldn't go off. I had a roan milk cow. She was curious and went up to smell that sack. About that time one of us hit it. I can see her yet. The blast picked her right up off the ground and spun her around in the air. When she came down, she was on her knees. She slid quite a ways. It was a wonder it didn't kill her. She never did give milk very good after that.

Joyce came out of the house and said, "What the heck are you doing?" Combustion from the blast had broken the windows out. It tore a door or two right off the wall. Dave was a baby, asleep in the crib, shards of glass covering him. Wanda's man got nervous and took off. Mosquitoes were thick. We had paste board on all the windows. Beings it was the 4th of July, all the stores around were closed. There was a man that had a hardware store in Wisdom. I called him, and after he laughed, he opened up his store. He cut 13 window glass pieces that day. Glen and I spent the rest of the day putting glass back in windows. Pete was supposed to come up in the next day or two, and I didn't want him seeing that mess.

*Joycelyn and Marilyn on the neighbor's Shetland.*
*Near Wisdom, Montana. August 1959.*

Pete was a little crinkly man that always smoked his pipe. One time he told me this story: He said he was a young boy traveling around the country. He came upon a farmhouse. There was a young couple there, who invited him in to sup. They said, "Come on in, we don't have much, but you are welcome to share the beans we have for supper." Later on that evening, them having only one bed, he crawled in with the husband and wife. The husband heard a noise, so he got up and went out to the barn to see what it was. While the man was gone, his wife said, "Quick, Pete, now's your chance!" So Pete jumped up and ate the beans.

Pete sold out to a fellow who farmed peat moss. He offered me a job, staying on to harvest that peat moss, but that didn't interest me too much. We had been there two years. We packed up and came home to Deep Creek.

# The Kelley Place

We stayed with Wade and Chloe Parrish that fall. We had too many cows to pasture after selling the Thomas Place, so we took them to some range on Pilot Peak. We sold cow and calf pairs for $150 apiece for a down payment on the Arthur Kelley ranch. I tore up all the fields and planted a good crop of alfalfa. I hauled it out to ranches all around to make Arthur's mortgage payment. The year was 1962.

*The Kelley Place taken from the west.*
*Note the Deep Creek Range and South Mountains in the background.*

Pete Johansen had some Hereford cows pastured at the Swallow's Ranch in Spring Valley. He decided to sell them to a fellow in Tooele who owned the merc. Lee Whitlock and I were hired to cut the tail end back that the guy didn't want. Pete told me to take the old cows and feed them that good alfalfa hay. I didn't have any money to pay for cows. Pete said that was all right, that he would take the steer calves when they calved out, and I would keep the heifer calves. We cut back cancer-eyed cows and some two-year-old heifers that were poor from calving.

Lee told me, "Jed, he's sweetening up your deal now." I got 65 head of cows. I had a grazing permit in the west hills, and the cows did real good. The cows all had calves. I weaned them in the fall.

Pete came along. I said, "Pete, let's cut your steers out."

He said, "No, keep them until they're yearlings; they'll bring more money." So I had 65 head of cull cows and 40 head of Herefords that came with the purchase of the Kelley Place.

Pete Johansen and Ray Skinner were so damn good to me. There I was, all set up, with their help. Ray would contract my calves and give me some money down to work on until the calves went. He'd say, "If you run out, come get you some more." Ray topped the market in Ogden with my calves several years in a row.

*Marilyn on Bud and Dave on Dandy. Circa 1962.*

Mother's homestead had 160 acres. Arthur Kelley's place had 260 acres. When Sherm Cook moved to Tooele, I bought his place that had 200 or so acres. The three places came with grazing permits on BLM ground to cover 150 head of cows and calves. I bought a couple of Charolais bulls just for novelty, but hell, they were lazy and wouldn't even look at a cow.

Dave and Marilyn went with me to Burley, Idaho, and bought four good Black Angus bulls. Everybody in the valley ran Herefords back then, and they were damn upset about me bringing home them no good Black Angus bulls. I guess they was afraid I'd contaminate the herds. I borrowed money from the bank and bought 40 head of Black Angus heifers from a guy in Ruby Valley, Nevada.

*Winter feeding with the skiff.*
*Joycelyn, Dave, Marilyn, and Jed behind a good team, Bud and Barney.*
*Circa 1962.*

When we were first on the Kelley Place, a vet came to vaccinate some of my heifers. One jumped out. It was winter time and slick. I saddled Ol' Blondie and went after the heifer. I made a lucky throw and caught her. Blondie spraddled out on the slick feed ground and kept his balance. He must have slid for 100 yards, but we kept ahold of the heifer. The vet said, "That is a pretty damn amazing horse, to keep his balance like that, and beautiful to boot."

*Joycelyn, Shetland pony, Dave, and Marilyn. 1962.*

*Dave and the Shetland. Note the Kelley Place house*
*and light plant house in the background. Circa 1964.*

101

*Dave and Les in the green floral chair. Circa 1964.*

Joycelyn showed Blondie in 4-H. She'd climb up on his back, and he'd stand as still as could be for her. She rode Ol' Blondie in the barrels at the Ely 4-H show when she was too young to compete. Back in those days, they set up barrels after the regular horse show events, and everybody competed. She ran Ol' Blondie around the barrels in fast time and won. The judges gave her the ribbon, but then took it away from her when they found out she wasn't old enough.

"That's all right," she said. "I'll come back next year and beat them anyway." And that's just what she did.

The next year, Joycelyn rode Buck at the Ely 4-H Show. He was about a three- or four-year-old colt. My mother was in the Ely hospital. I said to Joycelyn, "I've got to go to the hospital for a bit with your grandmother, but there's a girl from Vegas here that's pretty good, so come a-running."

I didn't get to see her run, but Charlie Baldwin was in the stands, and he told me the story later. He said he'd never seen a little girl use the spurs and ride like she did. He said she came out into the arena on Buck and spurred him good. When she did, he bogged his head and went to bucking with her. She hollered, "Buck, you son-of-a-bitch!"

The announcer said to the audience, "I hope you folks didn't hear what that little girl just called that buckskin horse."

Ol' Blondie's knees got kind of stove-up, so I sold him to Ray Skinner. Ray had bucking stock. One day, he was telling me about Blondie. He laughed and said, "He bucked those guys off in at the rodeo before God got the news."

Les was born while we were on the Kelley place. A few days before he was born, John and Gracian Auzquy, local Basque sheep-herders, had lost some sheep, and they came to the Kelley place and asked if I would help find them. I went to look for the sheep up towards Gold Hill. I heard on the radio in the truck that John F. Kennedy had been shot. Les was born a few days later, on the day Kennedy was buried. It was November 25, 1963. As coincidence would have it, that was Joyce's birthday too.

Les was a baby, and Joyce had diapers hung out on the line. Gene McCurdy was working for me, but this day he was going to help Sherm Cook with some cows on the mountain. He had a horse saddled up by the corral. When he got on, the horse bucked him off and came bucking up through the yard with the stirrups flapping. He bucked under the clothesline, and the saddle horn hooked on it, taking clothesline, diapers, and all. He bucked out south of the house in the sagebrush. I can see Joyce yet, gathering up them diapers scattered around. Once she had them gathered up, she had to wash them again in the wringer washing machine.

*Marilyn, Joycelyn, and Dave in the green floral chair by the oil stove where Joyce read to our kids. Circa 1962.*

The kids played with their horses in the hollows on the southwest side of the property. One day Les was riding Marilyn's mare Kazoomie. They had started loping towards home, and Kazoomie kept coming faster and faster. She come into the yard at a dead run. Les was about six years old. He fell off in the rocks. He got a hard bump on the head and was knocked out. I picked him up, carried him to the house, and laid him on the couch. After a while, he come to. His tongue started going in and out like a lizard. Joyce and I took the other kids to Lois and Walter's place and drove Les to town. He had a bad concussion.

One moonlit night, I saw steers in the north field where they weren't supposed to be. I jumped on my horse to push them back. Joycelyn come to help me in her pajamas on old Buck. Something spooked him in the moonlight. He stopped quick, and she fell off in a big puddle of water where I had been irrigating. She was wringing wet, but climbed back on and helped me with the steers.

Joyce was a gardener. I plowed a half-acre spot for her west of the house in that good black dirt. She planted corn, potatoes, carrots, peas, squash, cucumbers, radishes, onions, string beans, turnips, beets, spinach, and I don't know what else. I can see her yet, bent over, pulling weeds.

I hooked the kids' Shetland pony with the harness to the hand plow, and we dug potatoes. He was little enough that he could get through the rows without making a mess of the garden.

I dug a carrot cellar in the orchard. We filled it with carrots and covered it with a tarp. We had carrots all winter.

Joyce was a cook in more ways than one. She could make apple pies from the orchard that tasted like a piece of heaven. She made a carrot cake one summer. Culbert Pianum was irrigating for me, and he had come into dinner. He said he didn't like carrot cake, but when he tasted Joyce's, he damn near ate the whole cake.

She knew how to cook meat too. John Hamilton's wife taught her well. She Dutch-ovened lamb chops until hell wouldn't have it. She knew how to pan fry steak just right too. Her bread and rolls were real sweet and soft with a golden crust. I guess it was right that she cooked for the kids at school for over 10 years. They sure enjoyed her meals.

One summer day, Joyce sent me to Calloway's store for pectin and canning ingredients she needed. Wade Calloway was Wade Parrish's nephew. He come here from North Carolina after Wade came. He owned the store. Calloway was sitting up on the counter. There was a fellow there who was working in Ferber and a guy who lived in Gold Hill. They were drinking whiskey. The guy from Ferber was bragging about what a boxer he was. I heard the guy from Gold Hill say, "Yeah, well I boxed apples in Yakima, Washington, once too."

I laughed, went behind the counter, helped myself to the spices, and went on home. The next day I went back to pay Wade. He said, "Was you here yesterday?"

*Cook family ready to gather cows. Joycelyn on Blondie, Marilyn on Chris, Jed and Les on Slim, and Dave on Champ. Summer 1964.*

*Gerald Cook family at the Kelley Place. Summer 1964.*

# Ray Skinner's Death

My kids and I drove our cows to Ray Skinner's to spray them for flies. He had a sprayer on the back of his flatbed truck. The cows were in the round corrals. He had to do the spraying, so he was up on the back of the truck. He had just cut himself a piece of plug tobacco, when he fell dead off the back of the flatbed. We laid him in a little house on the end of the barn that served as a saddle shed. The coroner from Ely come and collected his body.

# Bringing Gracian off the Mountain

The Basque Auzquy brothers had a ranch in Nevada, but they had gone broke. They came to Deep Creek and leased Wade Parrish's grazing permit in the Basin of the Deep Creek Range. They bought some old ewes. They came here in the hard winter of 1948 and '49. Gracian died up in the Basin. John went out around the sheep. It was dark, and Gracian didn't come in. John couldn't find him. He finally found him the next morning, lying face down in the brush. John rode down here to the Kelley Place. He wanted to get a cop. John said, "I take the tarp off the bed, I kiss him and cover him, then I leave."

I took John to Wendover. Dan Fernanza was the cop then. Dan, Rao Bateman, John, a fellow from Ely, and I went up the mountain. By the time we got back up to the Basin, Gracian was ripe, blowed up like a cow. We rolled his body up in the bed tarp and put him on the horse. We tied him down like a deer carcass. I led the horse. It was August and in the heat of the day. Goop ran out of his mouth and down the horse's leg. When we got to the bottom of the canyon, we put him in a Jeep waiting there, and they took his body to Ely. I was pretty shaky in the belly after that. John gave me a fifth of whiskey. Rao and I drank it as we rode back down the bench to the Kelley Place. We'd get down on our bellies and drink out of the creek for a chaser. When we got to the ranch, we were feeling no pain. Joyce had dinner ready and waiting for us.

# Tobe, Pike, and Other Good Dogs

I got Tobe as a pup from Deverle Nicholes. He was out to sheep camp and had a dog that had pups. His dad Sid Nicholes imported those purebred Australian Shepherd dogs from Australia. I went out to visit Deverle, and when the visit was over, he handed me a pup up on the saddle. I was riding Ol' Pinto. That pup scratched the saddle, and Pinto went to bucking. I dropped the pup, so Deverle delivered the pup in his truck. He was a blue dog with one brown eye and one blue one. He was a damn good dog.

He went with us when we moved to the 3C ranch in Nevada. Joycelyn was a little girl and liked to play with him. He was getting a little old. A sore come on his head, and we thought it might be a cancer. We was afraid to let Joycelyn play with him, so I took him into Ely one day. Back of the courthouse, there was a big drum with a screen on the front. They gassed dogs in there. He went in and looked out at me like he wondered what the hell he had done. I didn't stick around. I sure felt bad. He was a damn good dog.

When we bought Arthur Kelley's place, I brought a black ring-necked heeler pup from Dillon with me. His name was Pike. He was a hell of a cow dog, and he'd kill a snake too. One time I was on the ridge west of the fields. There was a rattlesnake in a bush. I had got off my horse to find a rock and help Pike kill the snake. Well, the snake crawled out of the bush, and Pike grabbed it. Pieces of snake flew every-where. I was scared it was gonna go down the back of my neck. I went to buckin' and pawin' my head like a buckin' horse.

Me and my kids trailed our cows from the Kelley place through the hills to my mother's old place to rotate the pastures. The cows would string out along the wagon track that stretched between the places. There was a lot of snakes along that track too.

109

When Pike killed one, you'd better duck, 'cause pieces of snake might hit you in the head. After he killed one, Pike was skittish too. I'd take the end of my stiff rawhide rope and reach over and touch him with it just to tease him a little. He'd jump and walk on his two front legs for a ways.

I got a good bitch dog from Cliff Castagno in Grantsville. Pike and her had several litters of pups. At one time, I had given pups away all over this country. Alan Forsgren from Duck Water, Nevada, told me that one of those pups was the best damn dog he ever had. His wife said, when that dog got killed, Alan got down and cried like a baby.

Mandy Blue was a registered Australian Shepherd dog I owned. She was a long-haired blue merle with blue eyes. I sent her on an airplane to Twin Falls to be bred. The guy called and said he received her, but she jumped out and got away. I'll never know if somebody picked her up, or she got killed trying to get back home, but I never saw her again.

I've had some good cow dogs, and I've had some I couldn't make come back. I've worried I might get throat cancer from hollering at them.

Dick was a good Catahoula dog with that particular problem. Dick would chase a calf clear across the valley, especially if he had a helper. I'd holler and holler, and he would turn a deaf ear.

Them damn dogs of mine. If I ever do get to go to Heaven, I'm gonna have to holler, "Come back!" to my dogs.

# Nig and Darky

I bought a nice team of black Percheron colts from Harold Parker in Elko. They was still studs—about three-year-olds, I guess. I cut 'em first, and then I fooled around with 'em, broke 'em to lead, and put harnesses on 'em. I hooked them up one at a time to the buck rake with a wheel on it. They'd go around and around. I finally got them wore down some.

*Jed and Dave feeding cows with Nig and Darky. 1969.*

In my haystack yard, I had an old manure spreader that had been froze up and hadn't worked for years. I hooked the team up to that piece of machinery. Joycelyn was there helping me. I told her to entertain them at their heads, while I climbed into the spreader. I got in and tapped them with the lines. They took off and ran around the stack yard a few times until they saw the gate. Out and up through the sagebrush we went.

The manure spreader started coming unfroze. The teeth that push the manure back started turning. I was dancing over those things and trying to hold the team at the same time. Then the gears that spread the manure in the back came loose and started churning too. I worried that a car might be coming down the road and that I might run the tongue of the spreader through the radiator. Sure enough, here come Lois Weaver down the dirt road in her old push-button car. I managed to get them off the road enough so Lois could pass and into the tall sage brush where they finally stopped.

# In the Registered Horse Business

My cousin Jess Cook got me started in the registered horse business. In about 1961 or '62, he found me a stallion that had belonged to the Browning Cow outfit. This brown horse was a direct descendant of King. His name was Dark Chubby #40796.

*Dark Chubby AQHA #40796 and Jed Cook. July 19, 1964.*

I paid for him on time and leased three good registered mares. They produced some damn nice colts. Joycelyn's good horse Buck came from the old buckskin mare I leased. When Chubby got old, I traded with Earl Marshall in Tooele. Earl took old Chubby and made a hell of a lot of money breeding him in California.

*Branding and castrating a colt. Jed doing the castration, Dave at the head. Circa 1970.*

Earl traded me a registered palomino horse named Gold Spec #391025. I had him for a couple of years and got some more colts. He fell in a spring hole over to my mother's place one winter and died. Then I bought a sorrel horse from Wendell Castagno in Tooele. His registered name was Leo Bar Lu #455214. By then, I had a herd of 15 or 20 registered mares. Those Leo Bar Lu colts had a little buck to them.

In the '70s, I bought a palomino horse from Cliff Castagno in Grantsville. His registered name was Little Gold Nick #550438. He was a direct descendent of Nick Shoemaker #4119. My nephew in

Wells, Doyle Littledyke, leased me his mare Whiz Baby #P110,101. She was a phenomenal reining and working cowhorse mare that had won some titles. Her granddad was Chief #P-5. When it was all said and done, I guess I ran 30-40 mares over the years.

*Jed's 96 brand.*

115

**State of Utah**
**Department of Agriculture & Food**
Salt Lake City  UT  84114-6500

*Certificate of Registration*

Cattle/Horse

# 96

1-6114-00 RH
Right Hip

**GERALD W. COOK**

HC 61 BOX 6134
IBAPAH UT 84034

Is duly certified as the owner of the Brand,
or Earmark shown in the position or district
indicated. This certification is good until
transferred or until **12/31/2015**

Premises # 00E0SBL

*Utah brand registration. 96 on right hip.*

**State of Utah**
**Department of Agriculture & Food**
Salt Lake City  UT  84114-6500

*Certificate of Registration*

Cattle/Horse

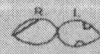

2-2P08-00 D2
District 2

**GERALD W. COOK**

HC 61 BOX 6134
IBAPAH UT 84034

Is duly certified as the owner of the Brand,
or Earmark shown in the position or district
indicated. This certification is good until
transferred or until **12/31/2015**

Premises # 00E0SBL

*Cattle earmark right upper slit and left upper and under bit.*

*Leo Bar Lu #455214.*
*Note the willow shed in the background where Jed got bucked off Slivers.*
*June 1974.*

*Little Gold Nick #550438 with the herd of mares. Circa 1975.*

*Jed's 96 belt buckle.*

*Jed wins Grand Champion Gelding Halter Class at Ely, Nevada, with Chubby Snicker Bar #2644029. August 1994.*

# Working Cows

I never did have much patience with dudes and fence sitters. When we branded calves, it was just me and my kids and oftentimes one or two damn handy Goshute cowboys. Gene McCurdy, Robin Bullcreek, Clark or Edmund Steele were all real good help. If Glen Pete was around, he was damn good help too, but he worked for a big ranch in Skull Valley most of the time. I always liked to wait until fall, when the calves had some good growth before cutting and marking them. We usually had between 150-200 calves to work. We used an alley and a calf table. It worked pretty slick.

*Jed castrating the calf. Joycelyn on Dusty, holding the rope tight. Dave assisting. Tie corral at the Audrey Cook Ranch. 1964.*

I branded with the 96 on the right hip. It was my granddad Jim Weaver's brand. He brought it here when he emigrated from England to Deep Creek in 1872. I also used my mother's brand, Quarter Circle C5.

Joyce always had a pot of cowboy beans and homemade bread for lunch. The next day or two, we'd have a good batch of calf oysters.

One time Charlie Baldwin came by after we had finished branding. I gave him some oysters. Dave was afraid he was going to take them all. Joyce sure knew how to cook them big oysters up nice and crisp.

In the summer of 1963, Dave and I were trailing cows from the Kelley Place to Grandma Cook's place through the hills. Dave kept wanting to lope his old horse. Dandy had been a real good cow horse. He sure knew how to watch a cow. He taught Dave how to ride, but he had ringbone and was stove-up. We were riding up a steep hill, and he loped up ahead. When I got up on top, the old horse was standing there, and Dave was knocked out, laying on the ground, blood running from his nose. I was riding a colt, so I threw my saddle on old Dandy so I could carry Dave. The blood was running down my leg as I held him. I thought if I could get to the creek I could clean him up some. I didn't want to scare Joyce. She was pregnant with Les at the time. I started to go through the back field to Hubert Steele's house, and Dave came around about then. He had a big bump on his head, but he was all right.

# Horseshows

My kids were horsemen. We went all over the state of Nevada to 4-H shows. They'd win the all-around title at the county show in Ely and then we'd travel to Fallon, or Gardnerville, or Las Vegas.

The year we went to Vegas, we drove right down Fremont Street with its fancy lights and sights. We were crowded in the cab of my old ton and a half blue Chevy truck with a wooden rack to hold the horses. We parked behind the Stardust Hotel. There was an arena in the rear of the hotel where the show was held. Moneyed people with their fancy outfits were parked all around. There were lots of contestants. My kids did all right. Joycelyn's old horse Buck could fairly skip through the western riding pattern. It was set up with some poles for the horse to maneuver through. He seemed to love that game. She won that class easy.

*4-H Performance Class. Marilyn and Kazoomie, on left.*
*Dave and Smokey, 4th from left, Joycelyn and Buck, 5th from left.*
*Las Vegas, Nevada. October 1971.*

The temperatures in Las Vegas were above 100 degrees. Joycelyn stood out there in an arena full of kids during showmanship class. When you showed your horse, you stood straight and tall with your knees locked most of the time. The class went on and on. One little gal, down the line from Joycelyn, fainted in that heat. We felt bad for that little girl. Joycelyn won that class too.

In 1970, we went to Fallon, Nevada, to the state 4-H horseshow. When we got there, we unloaded the horses from the truck, but found out we needed to relocate them the next morning. It was just coming light. Joycelyn was standing behind Sorrely in the chute. He had his head down, smelling and spooked of a shadow. About that same time, she swatted him on the butt, and he jumped and kicked her in the belly. It knocked her down and knocked the wind out of her. A.Z. Joy, the county extension agent for White Pine County, Nevada, was there. He ran over and picked her up. Luckily, her trophy 1970 White Pine Horse show buckle saved her. It still bears the bent marks from the horse's hind feet.

*Marilyn on Kazoomie winning a pleasure class.*
*Joycelyn right behind on Buckskin Chub. Ely, Nevada. 1971.*

Marilyn had a sorrel mare she called Kazoomie. I bought her from Earl Marshall in Tooele. She was damn hard to beat in the western pleasure class. Dave rode a good bay horse named Chris. Well, he rode a couple of other horses we had raised too. Their names were Smokey and Sorrely. He won his pleasure class, reining, and showmanship classes, too. I think those moneyed people were mad when my kids took most of the winnings.

*Les Cook won the Lead Line Class. Ely, Nevada. August 1970.*

When Les got old enough, he showed a horse I got from Jim Allen in Wallsburg, Utah. His name was Duster's Pop-up. We called him Duster. He showed him and a registered palomino mare in the 4-H showmanship, western pleasure, and reining classes. He also had a little sorrel horse we raised. We called him Country Bumpkin. Les showed him in 4-H too. Les was a damn tough competitor. I saw him ride a bareback out of a chute in Ely when he was in high school. He was scared and shaking, but damned if he didn't sit up there straighter than a string for a little ways.

One summer day, Les was getting ready for a horseshow. He had the halter on Duster and was going 'round and 'round. Duster was bucking and playing and Les was on the end of the halter rope. I was gonna tell him to get a longer rope. I drove over to the yard, and it happened just that fast. I turned around and Les was laying in the grass. Duster had kicked him in the face. My boy jumped up, running, blood squirting. I caught him and packed him to the house. I yelled for Joyce. She grabbed a dish towel and wrapped it around his face. We took off for town. His nose was split right down the middle. When the doctor had him on the table, I could look right into his head. He got stitched up and got all right. He couldn't pick the left side of his nose because the hole was too small for his finger.

If my kids weren't helping me with cows, they were practicing for 4-H classes. Just east of the house, there was a place big enough for a loping ring, cleared of sagebrush. They had some barrels set up there in the middle of the ring. In the evenings, they'd get their horses and go practice.

There was a yellow jacket nest in the corner of the Kelley house by the kitchen door. One day, when Dave was eight or nine years old, he went out the door, and a yellow jacket stung him between the eyes. His eyes swelled shut and got blacker than hell.

That evening or the next, the kids went to practice in the cleared spot. The dirt had gotten kind of dusty with all their practice. I can see Dave yet. He was running barrels on Chris. When Chris turned the third barrel, he balked and came home toward the corrals. Dave landed in the dirt. Poofer dirt flew up. His face was white with dust. His eyes swelled shut like that looked like two pee holes in the snow. "Chris, you son-of-a-bitch!" He bawled when he came walking back to the house.

Ely held a sanctioned quarter horse show for several years that drew lots of moneyed people, beautiful registered horses, and fancy outfits. It was called White Pine AQHA Horse Show. My kids competed there and took top honors much of the time.

*Les on Country Bumpkin (left), Marilyn on Stardust Heels (right).*
*White Pine Horse Show Stockhorse Race Ely, Nevada. 1979.*

The highlight was an event called the Stockhorse Race. Contestants lined up down the track on their saddle horses. The horses took off to a gunshot start. It was a quarterhorse race, 600 yards long. Several years, Marilyn won on her Starduster mare she called Maresy. One year, Les decided he'd get in the race on Country Bumpkin just to see if he could beat her. I've got the picture of the finish line here somewhere. Marilyn's mare was in foal three or four months. The picture shows the two horses running neck in neck, out in front of the pack, hell bent for leather. Les and Marilyn are looking at each other and laughing. Anyway, she beat the race. Les always said if the race was fifty yards longer, he would have won.

The kids competed in high school rodeo too. Marilyn went to state finals in barrels and goat tying on her sorrel mare. She tried out for queening too. She was a rodeo queen at the Bit and Spur rodeo when she was in high school.

Dave tried the rough stock, barebacks mostly, but I did see him ride a saddlebronc or two. He turned out to be a pretty damn good team roper. He never would have made it through school in Grantsville if it hadn't have been for a girl named Kelly Kinney. He had to keep his grades up to rodeo, and she'd end up doing his work for him just so they could team rope together. They went to the high school finals in Heber City several years in a row.

They showed their horses in horse shows in Tooele County too. Joycelyn and Marilyn won the buckles in the Western Pleasure class every time.

# Grantsville

Back in 1968, there was no school bus to Wendover. Joyce and I had talked to Maurice and Jane Brown in Grantsville when Joycelyn was in ninth grade. It was decided that she would stay with them and attend school. The night before school started, Joyce and I stayed in the bed, and Joycelyn slept in a bag on the floor. She bawled all night long. The next morning, I took her to the high school. She cried some more. Pretty soon, Duane Hicks come walking across the big room. He took her under his wing. She was all right then.

*White Pine 4-H Livestock Show winners from Deep Creek. 1970.*

The next year, we bought a split-level home on Main Street, so the kids could go to school. I took Dave to school the first day. I let him out of the car. He stood there on the lawn looking like a lost coyote amongst all those kids. When I drove away, I saw Morley Cook's boy—his name was Dave too. He walked up to Dave and took him into the school building.

*Joycelyn Cook with her 4-H lamb.*
*Al Littledyke, buyer. 1965.*

The kids went to the county 4-H show there in Ely. We'd haul lambs, steers, horses, and whatever they were going to exhibit in the buildings. We'd pack the livestock into the ton and a half Chevy and go over Schellbourne Pass on the dirt road. It was shorter than going down around to highway 93 by about 30 miles. Dave had a lamb that wouldn't fit in the back of the truck one year. The kids piled into the cab of the truck, and I lifted the lamb up on the floorboards. He rode that way all the way to Ely. Joyce would come along behind in the Suburban.

My kids did real good at the fair. Joycelyn has three or four grand champion steer trophies. She showed Hereford and Charolais-cross steers, but liked the Angus steers the best. Marilyn and Dave won grand and reserve champion too. One year, Marilyn had a black steer that was a snorty son-of-a-bitch. Marilyn probably weighed 90 pounds soaking wet. She was trying to lead that steer to show in the covered arena. He blew his nose and took off down through the corrals where the halter class horses was. I knew he was wild, so I had tied a lasso rope on the end of his lead rope. That steer dragged the county extension agent, A.Z. Joy, Jay Hicks, and me behind him. We finally got him stopped. If I remember right, that wild steer never did get judged, but Marilyn was able to sell him for a good price and ship him with the rest to slaughter.

The fair was a highlight of the summer. Everybody from Deep Creek stayed at the Grand Central motel in the center of town. After the day's events were through, we'd all have a toddy. Lois Weaver, Chloe Parrish, and Amy Hicks would have one drink and be dizzy and giggling.

When Jay Hick's girl Lori and my boy Les were four or five years old, they played on the grass in front of the rooms. They got curious about a phone booth that stood on the west end of the

128

building. They went in, shutting the door behind them, and then couldn't get out. We didn't hear them for a while because of the sound-proof glass. Poor little buggers were sure upset.

The kids sold their animals on Sunday. Basque and Ely businesses sure supported those 4-H kids. The kids would clean out the stalls and lead their animals to the semi. Some of the kids cried tears as big as horse turds when they loaded them, because they knew they were headed for slaughter.

It was always a sad time. Joyce loaded the kids in the car, kissed me good-bye, and headed for Grantsville to school. Dave would get so mad. He'd stamp his foot and cry, "School and money are the worst goddamned things ever invented." I'd load the horses on the truck and drive home. On the way home, we'd always stop at Schellbourne station and have a meal and visit with Lyman and Charlcy Rosenlund before we parted ways. It made the parting a little easier sometimes.

# Slivers

I bought Slivers from Jim Allen in Wallsburg, Utah. His registered name was Cinder's Duce. His sire was a horse called Duster's Duce. Some of them horses had a reputation for bucking. He was a tall, good-looking bay colt, weighing probably 1,100 pounds. I started to break him. I'd probably rode him four or five times. He was kind of snorty. I was home alone. Joyce and the kids were in Grantsville going to school. Some cows got in the field where they weren't supposed to be. It was late in the fall. There was five inches of snow on the ground.

I caught Slivers and jipped him around a little. I put the saddle on and was careful when I pulled up the cinch. He stepped off a few steps and went to bucking. It was slick in the corral, and he went down on his knees. I didn't get off. When he got to his feet, he bucked under the willow shed. I bent over backwards, and I guess I bent too far over the cantle. I hurt when he came out of the end of the shed. I throwed all holds loose. He bucked me off by the pole fence. I pulled myself up, but I couldn't walk. I thought my back was broke. I crawled on my belly and elbow through the corral to my truck. I pulled myself up by the steering wheel. I couldn't make my leg work for the clutch, so I put the truck in gear and popped the clutch to get it to go.

I drove myself to Edmund Steele's down the road a couple of miles. He came back with me and unsaddled the horse and turned the cows out of the corral. I knew I was hurt bad, so I was headed for town. I dropped Edmund at his house and went on down the valley to get Bill West to help drive me in. Bill lived at Parrishs' in Happy Jack's cabin. When I got there, I felt queasy, so I slid out of the truck and down on the ground. Rao Bateman and the local school teacher called the ambulance from Wendover. The teacher had a motor home. They helped me onto a chair and lifted me into the motor home. We met the ambulance between Deep Creek and Wendover. It really wasn't much of an ambulance, more of a closed-in pickup.

When I got to the LDS hospital in Salt Lake, they x-rayed my bones. I had a split pelvis. The doctors and nurses put me in a sling over the bed. There were weights on it. My butt never did hit the bed. I was in the hospital like that for a month. It sure broadened me out and cured me of the piles. I never had hemorrhoids again.

When I got healed up, I tried Slivers again. Damn, he was a nice horse. We had just branded a bunch of heifers, and we were pushing them around the fence by Merlin Johnson's plowed ground east of the ranch. I saw a heifer that we had missed. "Hell, kids, there's one we missed. I guess we ought to rope and at least earmark her," I said.

I chased her around in the sagebrush and got her kind of winded, so she wouldn't be so hard to hold. I made a lucky throw of the rope and caught her. Slivers went to bucking. I fell off, and when I landed, I landed right next to the heifer. I grabbed her by the front leg and held her down. My kids helped me. Slivers kept bucking right behind me. The stirrups were flapping up and down. I thought he would buck right on me, but he bucked down toward home. Joycelyn went and caught him on her horse. After I earmarked the heifer, I got back on him. It made me mad. I spurred him. Hell, you couldn't kick a buck out of him.

One weekend, Dave was home from school in Grantsville. We were going out in the field to look at some cows. He had Slivers caught. I said, "What the hell you going to do with that horse?"

"Ride him," he said.

We were standing down in the tall grass north of the house. I bent over to get a halter rope out of the grass. I heard snorting and bucking behind me. I turned around to see old Slivers and Dave going for a ride. He was sitting up there straight as a string too. Pretty soon, he fell off. He landed on his hands and knees in the grass. His nose was bloody. He didn't get up too quick. When he finally did get up, he said, "That son-of-a-bitch can buck, now!"

I asked him if he was going to ride him again, because if he wasn't, I was. He got back on him, and we rode out in the field. You couldn't kick a buck out of him.

One day I had him saddled up, leading him through the yard. Joyce said, "Why don't you get rid of that horse before he kills you?" I got kind of scared, 'cause I knew I couldn't ride him.

Stewart Sheldon drove in the yard one day. He offered to buy Slivers. I stood by the fence and scratched the dirt with the toe of my boot. I think I got $400 for him. Stewart sold him to a guy that roped around Delta. I saw that guy one time. He told me he won a roping on old Slivers and had a buckle to show for it. The next roping, Slivers bucked him off, and the roper said the horse damn near killed him.

Joyce and I went to Cheyenne Frontier Days rodeo years later, and I saw old Slivers in a corral of bucking horses. The rodeo was a three-night affair. I never got to see him buck out of a chute. I sure would've liked to.

I wrote a poem about Slivers.

# Me and Slivers

Once I had a horse we all called Slivers,
Sometimes, to think about riding him would give my old belly the quivers.
Slivers was a nice lookin' bay horse with lots of confirmation,
The bloodlines on his papers was straight from the Quarter Horse Association.
One day when I was home alone, no one around to see,
I thought I'd take a ride and if I got dumped there would be no one to laugh at me.
Slivers was a good lookin' horse, a horse anybody would be proud to ride.
But as I brushed him off, I got to thinkin', I had a shaky feelin' inside.
Slivers, he humped as I threw the saddle on his back.
I got the cinch and jerked the latigo to take up the slack.
I led him into a corral with a shed on one side so high.
Why a man would get on a bronc in here I'll never know why!
With a careful hand I took hold of the side of his head,
slappin' the stirrup leathers up and down.
Makin' sure he had all four feet well on the ground.
I carefully stepped up on Slivers with a smile on my face, when about that time I
thought we were both doing fine,
All at once Slivers grabbed his butt and hell did he unwind!
Me a fumblin' and grabbin' for somethin' to hold to and learnin' fast I wasn't tough.
When Slivers slipped and almost fell, damn I was glad 'cause I'd had enough.
Slivers quickly got his feet and he bucked harder than before,
toward the shed he did switch.
Me with my eyes buggin' out and pullin' as hard as I could, hollerin',
"Whoa, you son-of-a-bitch!"
We both went under the shed, me with my head bowed low,
Prayin' to God above to keep His hand on my head down here below.
He bucked out the other end of the shed and I was still on Slivers.
I knew then why, when I was brushin' him that my belly had the quivers.
We were both still partly together and I was wishin' Slivers would give up first,
'Cause I had a strong feelin' I would end up gettin' the worst.
Slivers bucked on across the corral, I had a feelin' he was losin' his pack.
Slivers and I parted company and I lit on my back.
Slivers kept on buckin' and showin' off, with stirrups flyin' high.
Me layin' there watchin' him and thinkin' what a damn fool am I.
I layed there 'til I got my wind and when I got up to go, my legs wouldn't work.
I stumbled, staggered, and fell. Oh hell, I knew by this that I was hurt.
I was layed up for about six months and as soon as I got back on my feet,
The first thing I did was get back with Slivers to teach him somethin'
and break him complete.

Slivers turned out to be a real good usin' horse
and to ride him cuttin' cattle was fun,
But Slivers never did forget how to buck and when he wanted to get you off
he knew how to get the job done.
Slivers was a good horse, but his disposition you never could trust.
Every time my wife thought I was goin' to ride him, she caused a fuss.
Slivers bucked me off several times and I never let anyone know,
My wife always preachin',
"He's gonna kill you, turn him loose, let the damn thing go."
One day a horse trader pulled in the yard,
Admirin' Slivers, he said, "To find a good horse is hard."
He offered me a price and after whittlin' and pawin' the dirt, I let Slivers go.
The last I saw of Slivers he was going down the road in the trader's truck
and where he went I'll never know.
Whoever wound up with Slivers, I hope gave him a good home
'cause he got a really good horse probably with no guarantee,
But there's one thing I do know, he better be a damn good hand
and a hell of a lot better bronc rider than me.

# Dummy

Old Dummy's registered name was "I'm A Duster." He was a damn nice cow horse, but was one of them good Leo Bar Lu colts that had a little buck in 'em too. It was deer hunting season. Stewart Sheldon and some other guys and me was riding the trail along on top of Bald Mountain. We had got off our horses to look around and was getting back on. I stuck my .30-30 rifle in a bush so I could get on Dummy. When I reached over to grab it, he blowed his nose and went to bucking. I could see the tops of trees. I held onto the rifle to the next bush. I stuck it in there until I could get him stopped. Whenever he heard a rifle shot or if one of those low jets would fly over, he'd go to bucking.

*Jed and Dummy working cows at Hick's ranch. Circa 1985.*

# I Quit Shaking Hands with the BLM

I've never understood how some pencil pusher could manage my land better than I could myself. I've dealt with BLM men most of my life. I will say this: the BLM guys on the Nevada side was a lot different from these guys over here in Utah.

A BLM man pulled in the yard one day to inform me that my herd of horses was trespassing on BLM land. I had been trying to bale hay, and my baler had broke down. I was parked under a tree, about half grouchy anyway. He said he was going to trespass me. I said, "Go ahead and try." Hell, he didn't even know where public land ended and private land started. I knew my horses weren't on BLM ground. We went the rounds for a little while.

One year, I had to get my cows out of Rocky. The permit was up. I didn't get five or six head. They were up in those trees we call the Doll. I could see them with the looking glass. I watched them for a day or two. They'd come down into Rocky Spring to drink and then go back up into the trees. When they finally come home, they were in the corner of the fence above Hibbard's place, and the gate was closed.

Decker and Kidd were the BLM men then. They happened to see those cows laying around by the corner of the fence before I got up there to get them. They drove in the yard, and Decker said he was going to trespass me. He was cocky as hell. He told me I wasn't honest. I told him to get off my property. He said he didn't have to go. I said, "Damn you, you will go," and I went in the house to get the gun. I meant to shoot under his feet and give him a little scare.

When I came back, he said, "I don't have to go."

"The hell you don't!" I said, and I smacked him in the face with my fist.

136

He went down. His partner jumped out of the truck to help. He had his arm full of papers. About that time, Dave come out of the house. He must have been 14 or 15 years old. Dave backhanded Kidd, and his papers went blowing across the yard.

"Will you bastards go now?" I said.

They jumped in their pickup and drove down the road.

And that's when I quit shaking hands with the BLM.

I wished I hadn't hit the guy, because it wasn't 30 minutes until everybody in the valley knew about it. Joyce's sister Blanche come up to the house. She told me, "Don't you know it's a federal offense to hit a government employee. You could go to jail."

I told her, "I don't give a goddamn. I hit him anyways."

# Reunions

The first Bates/Lee reunion was held at Frank Lee's place in about 1967. Mary Lee didn't really want it there again, so I said they could have it at the Kelley place after that. With all that lawn and the shade from the silver maples and willows, it was like a big park. Bertha and Charlie Baldwin, Ethyl and Domingo Mariluch, Earl and Elma Jones, Earl and Wanda Hibbard, and Lyle and Mildred Hibbard were just some of the reunion goers that showed up a week before and stayed the week after. People showed up with their campers, motor homes, and tents. Tents were pitched all over under the trees.

Picnic tables ran the length of the lawn for 100 feet or more. Food was always being set out and people eating and visiting around. Domingo ran a butcher shop in Ely. He would bring his special chorizo sausages and cook them. Charlie Baldwin cooked hot cakes every day for breakfast.

Times would get kinda wild. Somebody always had a jug. I gave $500 for a good Guernsey-cross milk cow. Harold Kelley, Clark Lee, and his brothers decided they were gonna saddle my milk cow and ride her. They put the Hamley saddle on the cow and rode her around the round corral. She bucked a little too. They spoiled my milk cow. I never did like to milk anyway.

When my boy Dave and Justin Parker were just kids, they found somebody's hooch. Justin's folks went home to Callao to do their evening chores. They come back and went to the dance, but Justin never showed up. He was asleep in Gilbert's cabin in the orchard. Dave made it to the dance all right.

We sure had some good music. My sister Mary was playing the piano in the front room, and Arthur Kelley was playing his fiddle.

People was crowded in there, laughing and listening and dancing. The house started to give away because we didn't have enough braces under it in the basement.

That same year, the second weekend in July, it snowed. Reunion goers crowded around in the unfinished basement. They set up tables, and everybody ate lunch huddled out of the weather.

We'd all dance 'til the sun came up. Saxons from Spring Valley used to play. Mrs. Saxon had tight curly hair. She got her exercise bouncing up and down on the piano bench. It's a wonder it didn't break. She was a damn good piano player.

My cousin Hans Williams, Ralph Severe, and a couple of other guys drove out from Grantsville to play for the dances for several years too. Hans could play any kind of an instrument, and he could set up on a bucking horse too. He probably only weighed 125 pounds.

Kids would be asleep under blankets, all over the linoleum in one of the classrooms off the dance floor.

They'd set out the school lunch tables in the dance hall of the school house. Everybody'd eat sandwiches and cakes for dessert. Then somebody would pass the hat, so the band would play longer, and we'd push the tables back and dance 'til the sun come up. Hans would play *"Turn Out The Lights, The Party's Over"* when it got light in the east.

# Teasing Joyce

We were married for 44 years and I don't believe we ever fought. Oh hell, I'd tease her a little sometimes.

I had a lousy heifer over to my mother's place one spring. She was weak and covered with lice. I was still getting over Old Slivers splitting my pelvis, so I was hobbling around on crutches. Dave brought her into the corral made of railroad ties to spray her. I went up to Ray Skinner's place to borrow some medicine. You mixed it up in a bucket. I told Dave to throw his rope on that heifer. He caught the heifer on a little palomino horse he was breaking. Joyce drove in the yard and got out of the suburban to help. She was wearing her heavy coat and overshoes. She climbed over the fence and into the corral. The manure was deep. The heifer seen her and made a dive for her. She couldn't run very good in those heavy overshoes. Dave had the heifer dallied by the saddle horn and the dallies slipped. The cow kept snorting and getting closer to Joyce. We couldn't help it. We started laughing. The heifer had her nose right on Joyce's heels. She turned around and hollered, "Doctor your own damn cow!" And she climbed over the pole fence and marched back to her car.

The Kelley Place had a good orchard full of summer apple trees, crab apple crosses, and hard green winter apples. There was even a plum tree. The trees were mature and the apples grew up high. Joyce wanted to pick some apples, so she climbed in the John Deere tractor scoop, and I lifted her up as high as the scoop would go. It was good picking, because she could put the apples in the scoop with her. I went down to the corral and started fooling with a damn colt. I forgot about Joyce and when I remembered, oh, it was probably a good two hours. I went back to the tractor and brought her down in the scoop. She wasn't too happy.

140

# Mustangs

I've always had a soft spot in my heart for mustangs. Hell, they don't eat that much feed. I sure have chased a lot of them. I remember chasing them with the Christiansen boys. Old Ned would be riding a perfectly good horse. He'd run right up in the middle of a bunch of mustangs with their bellies full of water. Then he'd bail off and ride a mustang by a mane hold.

Melbourne Robison had a brand-new Chevrolet. George Eldridge and him come over from Spring Valley. The Indians were trapping a bunch of mustangs and corralling them at Tippetts. They helped the Indians, driving that new car. Melbourne would run into the horses, so somebody could put a rope on one of them. One mustang jumped on the hood of the car. That brand-new Chevy was beat to hell.

*Gerald and Jelly Bean, a black mustang he caught. He'd buck every time he heard a rattlesnake, so Jed would tease him by reaching down, touching him on the neck, and hissing—just to make him buck.*

# Gilbert Rosenlund and Accomplices

Gilbert was a handy man, now. There wasn't much he couldn't do. He worked for me for a time and lived in the little one-room cabin in the orchard. He smoked leaf tobacco. Dave and Marilyn were kids. They'd sit and watch him get his paper out, sprinkle on the Prince Albert, roll it up, and lick it to stick. I'm pretty sure he gave them a sample more than once.

My mother's house was on the west side of the valley. I decided to move it to the Kelley place. Gilbert put it on some big timbers and moved it for me. He dozed a hole for the basement. He said he was in over his head when it came to laying bricks for the foundation, so we asked Punchy Christiansen and another fella from Grantsville to come and help lay the bricks.

Damn good brick masons they both were, too. One night, Gilbert and I was sitting at the kitchen table. Joyce and the kids were in Grantsville. We heard a car motor. It was quiet for a long time. All of a sudden, the front door flew open and in fell Punchy. The party was on then. Him and Gilbert went on for days. They'd drink and argue and drink some more. I got tired and went to lay down on the couch. I heard them talking and arguing. Punch said to Gilbert, "You know, Gilbert, a damned horse is the dumbest animal on Earth."

It was quiet for a minute. Then Gilbert said, "Now listen here, Punch, I don't believe you're right. A horse don't have to wipe his ass, and you do."

"I guess that's right," Punch said.

Gilbert knew how to move a house, too. Once he had my mother's white house beside the foundation, he put some timbers over the hole. He said, "Just touch the house, easy-like." The house rolled into place over the hole.

Earlier in his life, Gilbert lived with his wife Beverly and their kids on a place in Munsey Creek in Spring Valley. Beverly wore false teeth. One morning somebody drove in the yard, and Beverly didn't have her teeth in. She hurried and grabbed her teeth. Unbeknownst to Beverly, Gilbert had played a trick and switched out her teeth with old Fawn Henriod's teeth. She was a-gagging and a-spitting and couldn't figure out what was wrong with her teeth. Gilbert was just a-busting.

Harold Kelley and Gilbert Rosenlund drove in the yard one day. They had heard that the BLM had trapped some horses from down in the flat, and they were corralled at Tippetts. I jumped in with them, and we drove to Tippetts. It was a moonlit night. 15 or 20 horses stood in the corral. We decided to turn those horses out. Gilbert had a pair of fence cutters, and he cut the padlock on the gate. He went around to the back of the herd. I opened the gate. There was a shadow on the ground, from the shed in front of the gate, and the horses were scared to go out. All at once, one old mare jumped. Gilbert hollered, "Look out, Cook!" The rest followed her out. It sure was a beautiful sight, those horses running free in the light of the moon.

When Gilbert died, his family asked me to play my accordion and say a few words at his funeral. I said I'd play, but hell, I can't even talk to myself. Well, I stood up and said, "Gilbert's dead, and I might go to jail." But I told them that story anyway.

Gilbert was raised on a ranch in the north end of Spring Valley. One day in late fall, Gilbert's little brother went out to bring in the sheep. There came up a blizzard, and the horse came home without him. It snowed and snowed. Everybody searched and searched, but just couldn't find the boy. When it was spring and the snow finally melted, they found his body in the fields north of the house.

# Religion

I've never been one much for church. I believe that a man's God is in his heart, and when you're on a good horse in the mountains, that's when you're in the presence of God. I've seen God in action, when the storms roll in and the thunder and lightning cracks off those high canyon walls.

I joined the brotherhood of Masons 50 years ago. I belong to Rocky Mountain Lodge #11 in Tooele. I'm a 32nd degree Mason, a Shriner. Their motto is "Brotherly Love, Relief, Truth, Wisdom, Strength, and Beauty." Those are pretty good words to try to live by.

# Losing My Ranches

In 1973 or '74, I come in contact with a fellow by the name of George Smith. He worked for an outfit called Producers Livestock Loan Company. He and his son flew their airplane out to see my cattle operation. They were managing other ranchers in Ruby Valley and parts of Utah, too, so I fell in with them. Calf prices had taken a plunge. They encouraged me to keep my calves and feedlot them until prices came back and the calves were bigger. I shipped my calves to a feed lot in Burley, California. It went on for several years. Pretty soon, when the calf prices didn't come back, I couldn't pay my feed lot bill. I was indebted to Producers. Joyce and I were forced to sell the ranches to pay back George and his company. Some of those other ranchers lost their shirts to Producers, too.

So, I sold the places and had equity enough to buy a single-wide trailer house in Wendover. We moved it out to Wade Cook's property in Deep Creek. His boy Lance said we could live on the place. I had a few cows and sheep and a little herd of horses left. The place had a nice pasture to keep them.

I got a job with Tooele School District, driving bus for the high school kids going into Wendover. The job paid $10 for the drive in and $10 for the drive home. I worked for Glen Morgan, lifting bags of salt onto a pallet at the salt plant during the day. Joyce worked then too. She cooked in the kitchen at the elementary school.

Driving bus back then isn't the same as it is today. One time, two Indian boys were arguing and cussing at one another on the bus trip home. I pulled the bus over at Ferguson Springs and told the boys to get out. If they wanted to fight, I told them to have at it. They got off all right, and one boy popped the other in the nose, and it started to bleed. He started crying. I said, "Oh hell, if that's all you boys are gonna do, get back on the bus and let's go home."

My cousin Dan Rydalch was herding sheep in the flats near Ferber. One morning, he flagged the bus down and asked me if I'd bring him a jug from Wendover. I knew I might get in trouble, but I brought him a bottle anyway. I laid it under a certain bush so he'd know where to find it.

I had a push-button accordion, and I drove down to see him at sheep camp. His partner was an old guy full of arthritis. He come crawling into camp and laid down on the projection. Dan started playing his banjo, and I played my accordion. This old fellow jumped up and started step-dancing. Dan said, "I thought we was gonna have to kill him, but I believe he's gonna be all right."

One winter day, I come upon Edmond Steele sleeping in the barrow pit below Hicks' ranch. It was cold. I let him on the bus, and he went to Wendover with me and the kids. At the end of the school day, there was Edmund standing on the north side of the overpass, thumbing a ride back, so I gave him a ride home.

One New Year's Eve, I rode a palomino mare to Harold Kelley's place. It was just down the road. I bought the mare from him and wanted to show him how she was coming along. There was a big puddle of ice in the middle of their yard. I hobbled her front legs, so she'd stand while I went in to visit. She didn't know how to hobble, and she jumped and knocked me down on that puddle of ice. Then she fell on me. Joyce loaded me in the car and took me into my nephew Chuck Bean. He was an orthopedic surgeon in Davis County. The mare broke my left leg below the knee. He fixed it up with plates and screws. He told me he had only seen a break that bad one other time, when a fellow had been injured in an airplane crash. He told me, "Jed, that's a pretty bad break. I'm

146

afraid, when you get old, you're going to have some arthritis in it."
I guess he was right about that.

Joyce still had a share in the Parrish estate that Kyle Bateman now
owned and operated. When they bought her share out, part of the
payoff was a section of land on the mountains called Cold Springs.
We thought about moving to Cold Springs, but to put power and
electricity in would have been just too much money. So, we traded
the south end of the Cold Spring section for a parcel of land just
south of the old Kelley Place. We bought a double-wide trailer
house from a woman who lived by Calloway's store. She had only
lived in Deep Creek for a short time and had decided to go back to
where she came from. We bought her house and moved it to the
hill where it sits now.

# Mules

I've always liked mules. Once you've ridden a mule, you'll never go back to a damned horse.

The first mule I bought from a guy in Lake Point named Lenard Pearson. He said the mule was broke, but shit, he wasn't broke. He was a pretty little brown mule I called Jasper. He was kind of a snaky bastard too. I was riding him one time, and he bucked me, saddle, and all, off over his head.

*Jed and Jasper. 1986.*

148

Gerald Cook, resident of Ibapah, and his mule Jasper attended the Mule Days celebration in Fillmore over the Labor Day weekend. The festivities included a mule show, races, games and a parade. Jed and his mule took first prize for a single entry in the parade. It was a large gathering of mule owners and lovers, with some participants coming from as far away as California.

*Jed and Jasper.* **Tooele Bulletin** *article 1987.*

One time, I had him in a round corral down to Marilyn's place. I stepped up on him, and he went to bucking. Every jump he'd make, the damn dog would heel him. Pretty soon, I fell off. I lit kinda hard. Joyce had had a hip operation, and she was in a wheelchair up to the house. Our neighbor Mrs. Woodard was there visiting Joyce. She came down with her car. I crawled around and finally got up on the running board and into her car. Marilyn was teaching school. It was

149

Halloween. She come home, with her witch's outfit on, and took me to the clinic in Wendover. They had an old x-ray table there. When the guy x-rayed me, he said I had lucked out and only pulled a muscle. I laid around here for a month, on the floor or in the bed with pillows propped. I sure suffered. Marilyn's husband Pie scooped me up and took me into Holy Cross Hospital in Salt Lake City. Old Doc Weeks took care of me. He said, "No wonder you suffered: your hip is broke!"

While I was in the doctor's office, the nurse asked if there was anything I'd like... maybe a pain pill? Dr. Weeks came in and said, "Give him any damn thing he wants. Any man that is tough enough to lay around for a month with a broken hip deserves to get whatever he wants."

I saw a sorrel mule advertised in the classifieds of the Tooele newspaper. Steadman, that owned the motorcycle shop, owned him too. He said he bought a mare, and she had a colt in her. When it was born, it was this little sorrel mule. He said the mule was in Lehi. I called the guy in Lehi. He said, "Jed, I don't know what kind of a jack he's out of, but his mother was a hell of a good registered Poco Lyle mare. He's not a very big mule, but he'll be a good one."

I called Steadman and told him to mark "sold" on the mule. I think I paid $300 for him. He wasn't any bigger than my dog. We put a rope on each of his front feet. Pretty soon, he jumped into the back of the pickup. I had one of those closed-in racks. We stayed with Leo and Myrna Lee in Lehi. The mule was lonesome and brayed all night.

I brought him home and went to riding him. He was gentle and smart. I'd load him in the middle of my flatbed trailer and take him down the valley. He'd spraddle out. You couldn't throw him off.

*Jed and the sorrel mule at Fillmore mule days. Circa 1990.*
*Photo by Pam Olsen, Pro Photo Photography.*

I took him to Fillmore to the Mule Days' Celebration. He'd sidle up to the gate, and I'd open it without ever letting go of it; then I'd go through and close it. We jumped poles and obstacles in the trail class, and we won the reining and pleasure classes.

*Jed and the sorrel mule jumping an obstacle*
*in the Trail Class at Fillmore Mule Days. 1990.*
*Photo by Pam Olsen, Pro Photo Photography.*

He was handy to have around. I've roped off him and dragged calves to the branding fire. Dean Johnson was branding calves in Callao. I loaded the mule, and we went over the mountain. Buckaroos were playing at roping. It was taking a while. Billy Henriod said to me, "For hell sakes, Jed, unload your horse and help. We're gonna be here all day, if you don't."

People's eyes got wide when I unloaded my mule from the trailer. He was quick, now. I'd slick up the calf heels and take my dallies around the saddle horn. You'd better be hanging on, because he'd turn and go to dragging the calf to the fire.

He sure would get lonesome. If I went to the mountains looking for cows and I happened to get off him and tie him to a tree for whatever reason, he'd paw and bray and pitch a fit. I guess he was afraid I was leaving him there. But if I tied my dog there with him, he was all right.

Gail Parker had some cows on grazing permit up in the Dell. Gilbert Rosenlund and I went along to help him bring them home. We were riding along in the trees when, all of a sudden, a big white sheep stepped out. This sheep hadn't been sheared for two or three years. His wool was long. He blatted. My mule blew his nose, spun around with me, and took off. I couldn't hold him. I just held on and let him go. I would get him stopped, and then he'd turn around, and I'll be damned if that sheep wasn't following us. He'd turn and run again. I finally got him stopped by the lower reservation fence. The sheep must have got tired somewhere along the way and quit us.

Marilyn and I took a ride through Kingston's (Weaver's) alfalfa field one evening. She was riding her black and white pinto horse, and I was on the little sorrel mule. The kids called him Fitzgerald. I never knew his name. Sprinkler pipe lines were laid east to west in sections of the field. They were about three feet off the ground. To go from north to south, you had to go around the pipe or over. I said, "Come on, Marilyn, let's jump this sprinkler pipe." She didn't trust her horse and wouldn't do it, but me and the mule jumped over. I guess I was 80 then.

Joyce and I took him to Bishop, California, to Mule Days. I competed in the show with him, and while I was there, I bought another mule. She was a beautiful brown two-year-old registered mule. Her name was Lazy H Rio Dinero MMA 1443 (American Mule Registry).

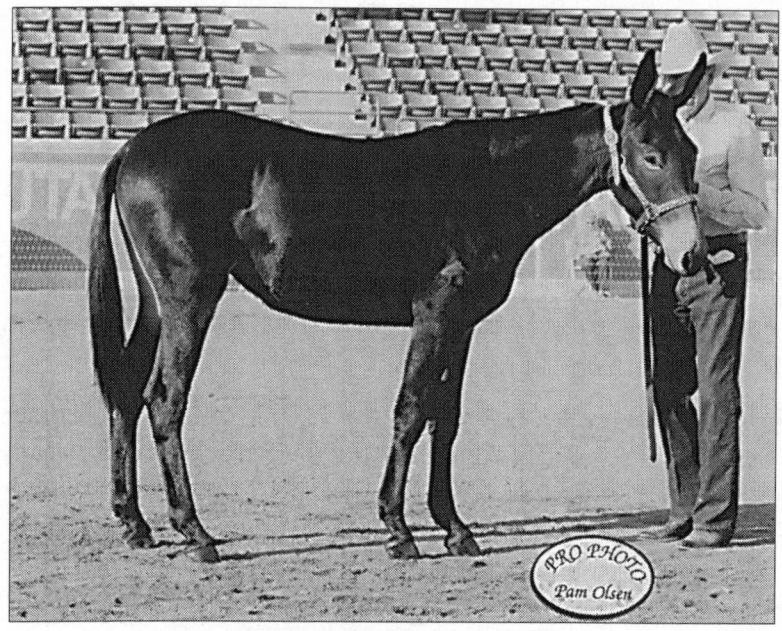

*Jed and Lazy H Rio Dinero. Fillmore Mule Days Halter Class. 1990.*
*Photo by Pam Olsen, Pro Photo Photography.*

She was a hell of a nice mule. I broke her to ride. She was a little snortier than the sorrel mule, but she sure could handle. Jay and Leatha Hicks came to visit, and I showed off my pretty mule for them. She had a good traveling gait. I rode through Marilyn's yard. Hicks were sitting on her porch. I headed up the hill. I don't know if it was a cat or a weed that spooked her, but she dropped her head and started bucking. All I saw ahead was ears. I stayed with her for a while, and when I unseated, I left spur rowel marks in the seat of the old Hamley saddle. Those marks were deep enough they still show up in the saddle's seat today.

# Losing Joyce

Joyce starting losing her ability to walk. She fell down a lot. We got one of those motorized wheelchairs for her to drive. She wasn't very good at it. The door frames in my house are gone from her running the chair into them.

When we'd go to town, she'd have to go to the bathroom. If we were out in the middle of nowhere, I'd get her out of the pickup and help her get her pants down. She'd get the giggles. I'd barely be able to hold her up sometimes. I'd have to help her in the women's restroom, and she'd get the giggles again. I guess it was because she didn't know what else to do.

She got to where she couldn't write or do housework or cook. Then she couldn't get dressed or feed herself very well.

*Jed playing,* **Have I Told You Lately That I Love You?** *Circa 1993.*

She'd ask me to play my accordion for her, and I'd play, *Have I Told You Lately That I Love You?* That was her favorite tune. It would cheer her up for a while.

I was out in the field when she had her spell. I came in to check on her. She was laying on the bed not able to talk. Marilyn called the ambulance from Wendover, and they took her to the University of Utah hospital. The doctors did what they could for her. Her condition always baffled the doctors. They called it multiple systems atrophies. She died three days later, on January 14, 2004. She was 67 years old. I lost the better part of myself when she died.

# Now

I kept 30 or so head of cows and a little herd of ranch horses until I was 90. I still have one old mare that I know I could ride, if I could get my leg over the cantle of the saddle. I rode in the National Pony Express Re-Ride up until I was 94, when I got too damn stiff to throw my own leg over.

Where I live overlooks the Kelley Place. The place is in ruins now, the log house, gone and the white house, shabby. The land belongs to the tribe and is leased to ranchers. I watch the cowboys bringing in cattle and taking cattle out. I see when they irrigate the fields and pasture the cows.

*Old friends, Jed Cook and Jay Hicks. Circa 1996.*

*Vit. "0" Cordyceps*

I don't go to the doctor very often. I take some good herbal supplements called Vitamin O and Cordyceps. Vitamin O is oxygenated water they get off the bottom of the ocean, and Cordyceps is a mushroom that grows in the high Himalayas. I've done all right with those supplements.

I tell Marilyn to bring me my smokes when she goes shopping. I've never smoked a day in my life, but I like those Cheetos. She cooks me a homemade hot cake smothered with butter and syrup and a real ranch egg almost every morning. I like chocolate Rice Crispy cereal on some mornings with whole milk and an ice cube.

*Jed and No News Just Whiskey 4319321.*
*He could ride her with two sticks to guide her and no bridle*
*after seeing a trainer do it on TV. 2008.*

The one doctor that I did visit retired. I've lived through two sets of hearing aids. The last ones wound up in the washing machine. I got new bottom dentures last summer, but I usually wear them in my pocket.

I lose my teeth from time to time. Awhile back I lost them and went around toothless for a month or so. My son-in-law Pie was changing the oil in my car, and the teeth jumped up from the corner in the oil box and bit him.

I sit in my recliner and reminisce about the old days. I watch TV with the sound turned up all the way, and I still can't hear it. I watch Let's Make a Deal. I go to church with Joyce Myers and other evangelistic preachers on Sundays. I enjoy Big Joe's Polka show, Molly B., and Marty Stewart on RFDTV Saturday nights. I talk on the phone to everybody I know who is still living.

*Jed. Circa 2010.*
*By Greg Martin Photography.*

My nephew Garn "Spanky" Littledyke has messed with music all his life. I remember when he was a little kid, and Mary and Sam came to visit from the Cleveland ranch where Sam was working. He picked up my dad's old violin and went right to playing a tune. He was a natural musician. He toured around the country with Chet Atkins and Waylon Jennings. He lives in Gardnerville and has a room full of guitars. He sent me some music CDs, and I enjoy listening to them.

*Jed playing his mouth organ.*
*Photo by Darby Linares Gebauer. 2012.*

I dream a lot. I dream of dead people. Stewart Sheldon and me are driving cows somewhere. My work horses broke through the fence into Walter and Lois' potato patch, and I was trying to drive them out. Wade Parrish and Floyd West and me going around the sheep. Jay Hicks had a tire with a big slice in it. He was jumping up and down on the tire, and the water was squirting out. I wake up hollering for somebody to turn my mules out with the horses.

*Jed at his piano.*
*Photo by Darby Linares Gebauer. 2017.*

I dream of Joyce. I feel her back up against my back, so real, as warm as can be. When I wake up, it's just the covers piled up on her side of the bed. I guess the electric blanket made it warm. Times like that, I wish I could go back to sleep and just keep on dreaming.

# Afterword

By Marilyn Linares

It is said that, to really find one's self, one must get lost in the middle of nowhere. In this case, by being lost in the middle of somewhere back in time, by unraveling the fabric of my father's being, I have rediscovered significant pieces of my true inner self, as well as rekindled forgotten memories along the way.

The aged log house stood in the shadows of giant silver maples and willows. Some trees towered over 50 feet high. In the evenings, my mother would gather us on the arms of a faded floral chair by the oil stove in the living room and read to us. We didn't have a whole lot of books. She read from a book called *All Horses Go to Heaven* or *Grimm's Fairy Tales*. Sometimes she would read a passage from the *Bible*.

We learned to chord on the piano and accompany my dad as he played his accordion. He'd tell us when to change keys. "Now change," he'd say, "Can't you hear that?"

I honestly don't think we could, as none of us inherited his natural musical talent.

My dad would fire up the "light plant" every Monday, like clockwork, so my mom could run the wringer washing machine to do the laundry. The tub had a dasher that, when plugged into electricity, gyrated to wash the clothes. After they were deemed clean, she would feed the articles of clothing, one at a time, through the wringer into the rinse tub. Once rinsed, my mother once again swiveled the arm of the wringer over the hang basket. She then fed the wet clothes through the wringer once again, to squeeze out as much water as possible. I remember feeding the clothes through along with my fingers sometimes. Thankfully, the wringer had a release knob. Joycelyn, Dave, and I helped her hang the clothes on the line stretched between two willow trees to dry.

My dad would start the light plant once a week, so we could watch the evening news with Walter Cronkite on our state-of-the-art, snowy, black and white Hoffman TV. I watched John Glen and Neil Armstrong make one giant leap for mankind as they landed on the moon on a summer night in 1969. I never watched cartoons and didn't even know what they were until much later in life.

It was necessary for my dad to go to Salt Lake City for supplies from time to time. Be it a load of coal or a load of cattle that brought him home late at night, mother and kids gathered around the kitchen table by the coal oil lamp and waited for him. Electricity hadn't made its way to Deep Creek yet. There were no yard lights, so the valley was completely bathed in darkness. We'd see a light far off in the distance to the north end of the valley. We'd watch the light slowly meander its way toward our kitchen window. Sometimes it was him. Sometimes it wasn't, and we'd wait again. Patience is a virtue learned early on.

We tied hay twine to Tonka trucks and pulled them in the front yard. They weren't just any Tonka trucks. These were trucks with gooseneck horse trailers on behind. The horses and cows inside had been properly painted and branded with a 96 to mimic our own steeds and herd. The roots of the aged willow trees were perfect for pretend corrals and ranches. We wore out a lot of twine.

One Christmas morning, my dad led a little dappled gray Shetland pony with a big red ribbon tied around his neck into the living room by the tree. He was such a cute Christmas surprise. Anybody that has ridden a distance knows that Shetlands are not quite designed for that. They take three steps for every big horse's one step, so they aren't very practical for cattle drives. But we did enjoy

162

him. We had a cart. My dad would hook him up, and Joycelyn would drive us to school with him. In the winter when his hair was long and shaggy, he looked like a silver teddy bear. We'd hook him to our Flexible Flyer sled and go for a sleigh ride. Snowmobiles of today didn't have anything on us.

When I was five or six years old, my dad had to make a business telephone call to the bank in Ely. The only phone at that time was at Tippetts' store some 20 miles to the west of the ranch. Childhood views are sometimes distorted, but I remember walking up the cement steps and opening a heavy door to a huge open space with groceries on shelves along the walls and a long white bar on the north end. On the east end sat a cubical white contraption unfamiliar to me. While my dad was on the phone, Bill Sellas showed me how to open the lid and view the strange contents within. He then helped me move a glass bottle along a track that snaked throughout the cube-like box. When the bottle came to the end of the track, I pulled it up and out of its holding trap. The bottle held icy cold orange liquid. I read "Crush" on the side of the bottle. Mr. Sellas helped me open the bottle top with an opener attached to the side of the box. I'll never forget the first time I tasted an orange soda pop, as the refreshing liquid slid smoothly over my palate and down my throat.

Dave and I rode two old bay horses known as "plugs." Bud was my horse. He was an aged bay gelding that had been a side benefit of purchasing the Kelley place. His top speed was probably five miles an hour, but he had a smooth old gait, and I felt safe on him. Joycelyn or Dave would often get on behind me and thump him in the flanks to make him kick-up. It was our country version of an equine roller coaster. Dave rode another old bay stove-up gelding named Dandy. My dad got him from Uncle Sam Littledyke. He was a retired roping and reining horse that had seen his better day.

When we drove cows from the Kelley place to Grandma Cook's place, which was at least five or six times a year, Dave and I brought up the rear, while Joycelyn and my dad on their younger, more athletic horses took the lead or the flanks of the herd. If it was summer and the weather was particularly dry, Dave and I were often practically invisible in a cloud of dust at the tail end with the stragglers — our faces, hands, and Levis covered in a thick coating of clay, our throats mighty dry. We rode postage stamp-sized saddles atop these two old plugs. The saddles were as old as time, and the leather on both horns had come unstitched, leaving the top piece of leather to freely flap up and down. Dave and I used to pretend that an orange crush magically appeared from under the leather flaps to quench our thirst.

One television show we did have knowledge of was *Gunsmoke*. We were drawn in by it so much that we became the characters in our play. Joycelyn was Matt Dillon with her buttermilk buckskin horse, and Dave became Festus Haggen complete with jingling spurs and slouch hat. His mustang horse Champ substituted for Festus' mule. Les was Doc because he was too little to have a horse yet and had to stay in town, aka the log house. I was Miss Kitty, and I'm not sure why. We constructed elaborate camps in the sagebrush and greasewoods east of the ranch. The junkyard over the hill provided the essentials for setting up shop. We'd lose track of hours playing *Gunsmoke*.

My grandkids will attest to the fact that some artifacts still remain. On a recent exploration, we came across the remnants of a turquoise dish drainer and a rusted granite coffee cup. The years fell away as I immediately recognized Miss Kitty's camp.

The Kelley place land has two deep hollows, or arroyos, running north to south on the west side of the property. Along the steep edges of the hollows, as well as on the sides, there grows sagebrush higher than my head while on horseback. The shelter of the hollow, coupled with ample sagebrush building material, created the perfect set of circumstances for building hideouts, complete with corrals for the horses. Joycelyn, Dave, and I were so enthralled in that particular activity one summer day that we lost track of the hours. It became moonlight, and even then, we never looked up from our engineering endeavors. Suddenly, we heard the roar of an engine, and the headlights of my dad's pickup shot eerie shadows across the walls of the canyon. My mother, my grandma Audrey, and he were squeezed in the cab with serious looks upon their faces. We knew, without any words being spoken, that we were in trouble then.

My dad wasn't too much on carrying essentials like water and snacks. I do remember having Vienna sausages—he called them baby dinks—and soda cracker crumbs, squished from the saddle bag.

My dad had a grazing permit for our cows in the Basin and the Dell on the Deep Creek Mountains. On one occasion, it got late and then grew dark before we could get home. We spent the night under the stars with our heads in our saddles, covered by our saddle blankets. When we rode into the ranch in the morning, Mother had a big stack of hot cakes, bacon, and eggs ready for us. Food never tasted so good.

Because Joycelyn's horse Buck had a set of shoes on and it was rocky up the Rocky Canyon, Dad decided to pack him with camping supplies one time. Dad headed out of the yard with Buck loaded down with full saddle bags. We trailed behind him. When he led Buck through the brush, the metal utensils rattled. True to his name, he spooked and went to bucking. He scattered knives and forks and toilet paper through the brush until hell wouldn't have it.

165

Dad's sayings I pass on to my kids:

- I don't mind the smell, but the stink hurts my eyes.
- Get up and pee; the world's on fire.
- If you get tired of walking, run a ways.
- That smell would knock a dog off a gut wagon.
- Sitting up straight as a string.

He'd sing little old songs to us kids when it grew quiet and we were tired and a-horseback. I've sung his songs to my children and grandchildren. Here's a few:

*A Pat on the Back*
*Give yourself a pat on the back, a pat on the back,*
*a pat on the back and say to yourself with jolly good health,*
*I've had a good day today.*
*Yesterday was full of troubles and sorrow.*
*You never can tell what's gonna happen tomorrow.*
*So, say to yourself with jolly good heath I've had a good day today!*

*Hallelujah, I'm a Bum*
*Hallelujah, I'm a bum, hallelujah, bum again,*
*Hallelujah, give us a handout to revive us again.*
*I went to the house and I knocked on the door.*
*The lady said, "Bum, bum, you've been here before."*
*Hallelujah, I'm a bum, hallelujah, bum again,*
*Hallelujah, give us a handout to revive us again.*

*Poor Folks*
*Poor folks, poor folks, we ain't nothin' but poor folks*
*Poor folks livin' in a rich man's world*
*Sure was a hungry bunch.*
*If a wolf a-comin' a-knockin' on our front door*
*He'd have to bring along a pic-a-nic lunch.*

166

*Team of Horses*
*Dave (or insert name here) had a team of horses,*
*The best that you could find.*
*He also had a driver with a wagon on behind.*
*One dark and stormy night, he got his best horse stole*
*He could not find that horse, though he tried with all his might.*
*Now Marilyn (or insert name here) being a Christian*
*Said to Dave (or insert name here) one day,*
*If you want that horseback, you better get down and pray.*
*Now Dave thinking she was right, got down and prayed, of course,*
*Sure enough, that thief came back and stole his other horse.*

My dad says he doesn't ever remember getting in an argument with my mother. I will attest to that fact. They were too busy trying to make ranching work, working side by side. They were pretty good partners. However, I do remember when one particular reunion dance ended along towards sunup, and my mother helped my dad into the rear section of her Chevy Suburban. He had previously partaken of too much libation. The seats had been laid down, creating a make-shift bed for my dad. The back of the seats were hard plastic. Hex bolts secured the plastic to the front of the seat. He curled up on that surface for the ensuing ride home.

I was 12 or 13 years old. My brothers and sister were there too. I sat in the front seat, but I heard the faint thump of my dad's head occasionally hitting a bolt in the back of the car, as my mother rather knowingly aimed for the deep ruts in the dirt road home. The next morning, my dad sat on the unlit wood cook stove with his head in his hands. My mother's small twinkle in her eye and her slight smile let me know she knew she had, in a small way, contributed to his temporary self-inflicted pain.

Jed was a regular Pecos Bill with livestock. He could fix anything that had hair on it. With other handyman tasks, he wasn't quite so inclined.

When Les was born, Aunt Mary came to stay with us. She was disgusted with the fridge. The pot metal handle had broken off some time ago. The seal was also broken. My dad's solution to the problem was to drill a screw into the side and keep it closed with a piece of inner tube stretched around. You opened it with a screw driver that slept on top of the fridge when not in use.

After Gilbert and Punchy completed the bricking, Gilbert moved Grandma Cook's white house from the west side of the valley. It was in need of steps by the south kitchen door. My dad's solution was to place two long eight-inch pieces of lumber across the cavern of unfinished basement to the safety of solid ground some 15 feet away. We walked "the plank" for 10 years.

That white house didn't have running water or a bathroom. We carried water and used the outhouse throughout our childhood and teenage years. There was a big celebration in 1979. Some people may remember my wedding, but it was just as big a deal to get the indoor plumbing fixed.

Dad shot his house once in 1988 or '89. A woodpecker was annoyingly pecking holes on the south side of his house. He sneaked out the backdoor intending to make short work of the bird. According to his account, his arthritic thumb let go of the stiff hammer on his granddad Jim Weaver's old 12-gauge shotgun, and he sprayed the west wall with buckshot. The bird flew away. Dad split his thumb open from the ordeal. He went inside to survey the damage. Thankfully, the pellets missed Joyce and the clothes dryer, but they perforated his bathtub and spun around the oval tub as if it was a BB race track. The buckshot sprayed the shower curtain full of holes. The tub still bears the marks, but is "temporarily fixed" with duct tape. The peek-a-boo shower curtain still hangs limply like a wounded woodpecker.

The doorknob on the back side of his house ceased working effectively. Every time the wind blew, the door flew open. He remedied this problem easily, by tying a lasso rope around the handle on his oven door, around the foyer, and securing the door handle on the inside. With a half-hitch, the rope stretched tight and quickly solved the immediate problem. He was quite proud of his ingenuity, and the door stayed shut with the rawhide rope, until someone more mechanically inclined came along and fixed it in a more conventional fashion.

There were things he never learned to do. He never learned to ride a bicycle. He never learned to swim. He used to tell us kids that he dived like a feather and swam like a rock! When he was 80 or so years old, he went with his good friend Linda Clayton to the Caribbean Islands. One day, they took a little boat out into the harbor, and Linda dove off the side for a dip in the water. "I was scared. I knew I couldn't save her if she started drowning, but hell, she could swim like a fish," he said.

He's been in a movie theatre two or three times in his life. I remember him taking us to Old Yeller one time and Sound of Music another. Those were the only movies I saw in a show house as a kid.

Several years back, he flew with me to Las Vegas. I had a teachers' convention, and he went along to visit his friend Linda. As we were going through security in the Salt Lake City Airport, he set off the device. Due to his internal metal plates in his leg and screws in his hip and knee, he got the thorough once over, complete with removal of outer garments and pat-down from security personnel. I thought to myself that, in today's world, security should be tight, but I couldn't imagine how the employees could envision his bent old frame being capable of hijacking an airplane.

When terminology either becomes obsolete or futuristic, conversations become difficult. As an example, when he talks of wagon burrs or Jackson forks, I have limited vision for what they mean, but get meaning by the context in which they are used. The same holds true for him. A technological conversation with Jed would be near impossible to have. To him IPads are a home remedy patch for sore eyes. IPods are a new brand of pea seeds for the garden. Apple is sweet green summer, hard red winter, or crab apple-cross variety that grew in our orchard. Dell is a grazing permit below the Basin where he pastured cattle.

I don't believe he's ever sat through a ball game of any kind. He'd pretty much interrupt anything to go to a rodeo, but ball games never held his interest. I recently had a conversation with the satellite TV billing department. They were charging him for the "premium sports package." It was quite a large bill, especially for an old man living on social security pension. The receptionist explained that he had not called into to say he didn't want the premium package and so it automatically took effect. It apparently could not be cancelled until "March Madness" was over. I explained that Mr. Cook had never watched a basketball game in his life and had no idea what March Madness even was. The conversation escalated, and soon I was talking to the manager. Needless to say, the "premium sports package" was subsequently canceled.

He quit driving on Memorial Day 2016. He had several instances where he had "gotten stuck," and as luck would have it, someone was always around to rescue him and his '92 Crown Victoria. Deep Creek cemetery is a picturesque country cemetery complete with do-it-yourself caretakers. My family had spent the day raking weeds and tidying family graves. Towards sundown, my dad drove in the gate. The cemetery has a drive-through path for visitors. My dad drove along the path. When he got up on the hill, he became disoriented and tried to turn around. There is not ample room to turn, and subsequently he knocked two headstones askew. He stopped, high-centered on a headstone. It strikes me as quite ironic that the grave he chose to accidentally drive over was that of his good old friend, Happy Jack. Pie and I ran to stop him from doing further damage. I said, "Jed, stop! You ran over Happy Jack's grave!" The car door dinged as he bent out behind the wheel and asked, "I did? How old was Old Happy Jack anyway?"

Along with his brilliant memory of long ago, he keeps his wit and spunk. One particular visit to the emergency room last year had a nurse asking the question, "Mr. Cook, do you feel safe at home?" She was referring to safety issues and the threat of falling. He construed a different meaning of the question when he replied, "I feel a damn sight safer at home than I do in this place." She laughed and asked if she could type that in the records.

He was recently hospitalized with a urinary tract infection. He became very ill for a couple of days. On the second day, he contemplated a nursing home, but by the third day, he was his feisty self. The physical therapist walked him and his walker around the floor. She told him to turn left to go back to his room. He lifted his left hand in the air. She was startled and told him to put his hand back on the walker. He told her he was just signaling.

I like to believe that Jed's and Joyce's kids grew up to be decent, hardworking people. Joycelyn and her little dog Rags reside with my dad. She has two beautiful daughters and three even more beautiful grandchildren.

Dave lives in Wendover with his bride Evelyn. They have three beautiful grown children and three even more beautiful grandchildren. When he's not working at his regular job with Nevada Department of Transportation, Dave shoes horses for practically every horseman and woman in Elko County. He is the cowboy extraordinaire in the spring, when there's branding to be done, and in the fall, when there's gathering or doctoring or anything to do with cattle.

Les flew farthest from the nest. He moved around the country a bit and eventually landed in Houghton, Michigan, with his wife Stephanie. He is Vice President for Student Affairs and Advancement at Michigan Technological University. They have two beautiful grown children.

I am blessed to live within the sound of Jed's accordion and mouth organ music. On summer nights, he occasionally leaves his windows open, and the melody floats down the hill. I enjoy riding my horses in the mountains. I've always had a fetish for paint horses. I bought a good stud and raised a few good colored colts, so if you have inclination to see a horse of a different color, look no further than my corral. I've spent the past 30 years as an elementary school educator, but retired in June 2016. Pie and I have three... and for want of a better adjective... beautiful children and three even more beautiful grandchildren.

The tales of our families, together with their joys and sorrows, their trials and triumphs—quite possibly as intriguing and unbelievable as my father's—are stories best saved for now and are waiting to be written on yet another God-given day.

# The 96

By Marilyn Linares

*It came with young James Weaver and his wife, Annie*
*To Ibapah they immigrated from the old country and homesteaded in the valley.*
*Just a simple piece of rusted iron bent in a peculiar shape.*
*But oh, what a story and oh what a legacy, to have and to cherish and to keep.*
*Jim Weaver was my dad's granddad.*
*The 96 was the brand he carried as a young lad.*
*The year was 1872 when they settled here to stay.*
*Times were tough, he raised kids, and sheep and hay.*
*He branded his stock with the 96 way back in long ago yester year,*
*He grew old and passed the brand to his son Lester to mark his heifers and steers.*
*Lester worked for Wade Parrish and kept a few cows there.*
*He branded their hide with the 96 to keep things fair and square.*
*Time passed and Lester grew old as people will sometimes do.*
*Although he had used it for quite a while, with the brand he was through.*
*He passed the brand to Jed's brother, Les to have and to use and to keep.*
*Les continued to use it to mark his cattle, horses, and sheep.*
*He was a horseman, his reputation by folks around, quite well known.*
*He traveled on early from this world and left the brand for Jed to own.*
*For sixty years or possibly more Jed has marked his stock.*
*With that neat little brand, the 96, showing up on the right side, plain as chalk.*
*With that brand, the 96, my dad takes lots of pride*
*He has said time and again, how nice it shows up on a cow's back side.*
*I can see him yet with the brand in his hand doing his cowboy work*
*Through a plume of burning hair, he'd stand back from the calf*
*And brush the singe away.*
*Pushing his hat back from his sweaty brow*
*He'd say now there's a brand that shows up on a cow!*
*Time has passed and people get old as fortunate people sometimes do*
*The brand rests, hanging on a nail now not much to do.*
*But the story goes on and so will the brand I'm certain of that*
*That neat little piece of twisted iron, branding the cattle fat.*

# About the Author

*Marilyn Linares and her good gelding, Spud. 2014.*
*Photo by Mike Ringholtz.*

Marilyn Linares has lived most of her life in Ibapah, Utah. She has always had a love for books and book making. She attended Grantsville High School where she was the yearbook editor. She received her Associate of Science from Dixie College and her Bachelor of Science in Elementary Education from University of Utah. During her 30 years as an elementary educator, she was involved in the following book projects:

**Co-authored and co-produced,**
along with Goshute Elders and teachers:
*Pia Toya, A Goshute Indian Legend.* 2000. *University of Utah Press.*
**In conjunction with Goshute Elders, she helped produce:**
*Aipimpa, A Celebration of Water. 2011.*
**She wrote, and her students illustrated:**
*My Pony Express Trail,* a children's book featured in *Echo of Hoofbeats, The Pony Express Story* by Hal McClure Productions. 2004.

She is a member of the National Pony Express Association. She is married to Al "Pie" Linares. They have three adult children: Haley, Darby, and Will. They also have three grandchildren: Bohdan, Gerald, and Sienna. Marilyn spends her days visiting with her father and her family, and tinkering with her horses.

# About the Editor

A native Montanan, Nancy was raised on her family's ranch east of Billings, Montana. She and husband Scott home-schooled their children, Stephanie and Luke, who were awarded scholarships at Notre Dame and University of Oklahoma. Nancy attended Rocky Mountain College, earning her Bachelor of Science in Applied Management. After 20 years of working and plumb tired of town, she quit her job to focus on what she loves. A self-described jack-of-all-trades, she has been interested in almost everything that came her way. She edits, writes books and poetry; makes cowboy ceramic dishes; paints; sews, designs jewelry, and plays piano, flute and guitar. As writer, editor, co-editor, designer, typesetter, and/or illustrator, some of her projects include:

*Makin' Tracks, With My Horses and Mules, by Jane Lambert, 2017.*
*Finding Her Place, A Harper Anthony Novel, by Nancy Morrison, 2017.*
*This Land on Indian Creek, by Nancy Morrison et al., 2017.*
*Making Fun with Family* (working title), *by James E. Walker, 2017.*
*Aubry Smith's Cowboy Art, by Aubry Smith, 2016;*
*Wolves At Your Door, by Earl Stahl, 2016;*
*Growing Up, Writing Down, Volumes I-III, by Al Anderson, 2016;*
*Displaced, A Harper Anthony Novel, by Nancy Morrison, 2015.*
*The Real Wolf, by Lyon & Graves, 2014;*
*Since the Days of the Buffalo, by Michael Bugenstein, 2013;*
*As I Saw It, A Biography of Pat Goggins, by Linda Grosskopf, 2013;*
*Charlie Russell: The Cowboy Years, by Jane Lambert, 2011.*
*The Weak Ones Turned Back, The Cowards Never Started: A Century of Ranching in Montana, by Linda Grosskopf, 2009.*

Made in the USA
San Bernardino, CA
18 July 2017